SOLVING
Hard Conflict

A Practical Guide for Organizations of All Sizes

ANGELA RAMSAY PhD

LMH
LMH PUBLISHING LIMITED

Executive Editor: K. Sean Harris
Cover Design: Sanya Dockery
Book Design, Layout & Typesetting: Sanya Dockery

Published by LMH Publishing Limited
Suite 10-11
Sagicor Industrial Complex
7 Norman Road
Kingston C.S.O., Jamaica
Tel.: (876) 938-0005; 938-0712
Fax: (876) 759-8752
Email: lmhbookpublishing@cwjamaica.com
Website: www.lmhpublishing.com

Printed in the USA   ISBN: 978-976-8202-90-1

NATIONAL LIBRARY OF JAMAICA CATALOGUING-IN-PUBLICATION DATA

Ramsay, Angela
    Solving hard conflict : a practical guide for organizations of all sizes /
Angela Ramsay

    p. ; cm.
Includes index
ISBN 978-976-8202-90-1 (pbk)

1. Conflict management
I. Title

658.4053 - dc 22

Other Titles by Angela Ramsay

Community Development Strategies
University of the West Indies

Adult Education in the Caribbean at the Turn of the Century
UNESCO

Understanding HIV/AUIDS and Drug Abuse
UNESCO

We Can Stop Violence
UNESCO

Help for Anxious People
UNESCO

The Dilemma of Science
Ian Randle (UNESCO supported)

Good Practice in Achieving Universal Primary Education
Commonwealth Secretariat, London

Table of Contents

Introduction

Conflict is a master robber of energy. I learned this at age sixteen when I convinced a young woman not to take a weapon to an unfaithful lover: not because I was that skilled in managing conflict – I was just lucky! The families of the two participants had engaged in verbal battles for years, a local illustration of conflict's aggressive reproductive ability. From the global perspective, wars lead to other wars: to illustrate, The Korean War erupted partly because certain issues during World War II were unaddressed.

Think of hard conflict as a clog, thick and grimy. In this book, conflict refers to the clog placed in the arteries of an organization, robbing employees of productive energy. Employees may not sleep well at night, plot schemes to avenge perceived wrongs, or be overcome by the spectre of learned helplessness. They may not expose their feelings at work: an employee can laugh with a colleague at lunch and undermine him ten minutes later. But conflict is not just about negativity. If we take another look at World War II, we see that that major conflict generated the creation of new and important technology.

Thankfully, there are exciting ways to stimulate creativity without the suffering associated with the loss of anyone's family member, and in the case of the workplace, without debilitating emotional and physical health. Clearly, we need conflict for stimulation and creativity, sometimes referred to as "creative" or "constructive" tension, and organizational leaders can use this form of tension to their considerable advantage – to exploit the great novel ideas that would not have been spawned were life too comfortable. It has been argued that companies such as General Motors, Eastern Airlines and K Mart stagnated in past decades not because they had too much conflict, but because management became complacent and unwilling to stimulate the change required.[1] In certain cases, complacency is a cousin of conflict. We just can't be bothered because the system can't be changed anyway: why tire ourselves out with all this change management stuff when our colleagues are intractable or the pay is so small!

The positive relationship between less conflict and greater productivity has been established. For example, the number of cases of conflict being reduced at Motorola positively correlated with the increase in sales.[2] Organizational structures, cultures and systems generate or reduce conflict. But even if every preventative measure exists to allow organizational citizens to better concentrate on their work and be happier generally, conflict will make itself felt from time to time. Conflict arises when people with unmet needs have different purposes, perceptions, personalities, prior experiences and problems, a medley of Ps that creates miscommunication, insensitivities and hypersensitivities – and a messy competition for resources.

It's better to prevent conflicts in the first place, and prevention is facilitated when both leaders and followers understand the most important kinds of work conflicts and engage in wise and constructive narrative about the issues and how they may be solved. This book addresses conflict in general, and also discusses three forms of hard conflict. To this end, Chapter 1 focuses on the under-standing of three types of hard conflict: undermining, bullying and violence. Chapters 2 to 8 discuss practical interventions that reduce all forms of organizational conflict, and also provide specific recommendations for bullying, undermining and physical violence.

Hard conflict is prevalent, and in times of job scarcity, many executives, middle managers and other employees feel that they must tolerate bullying, or work in environments shrouded in covert political behavior. The exciting news is that conflict can be prevented, and even be ameliorated to the point of reconciliation. But it is more than that. Constructive conflict can be used to generate brilliant ideas. Conflict is like dough - shaped as a dagger or land-scape. This book looks at the reshaping of conflict as an energized work of art.

CHAPTER 1

Understanding Three Types of Hard Conflict

E ven the best learning organizations have disharmony within their walls. Large organizations are also receptacles for conflict, unless all forms of disharmony are closely monitored and addressed. Lack of admission that hard conflict exists only serves to embed disharmony in the workplace.[3]

Even one "conflict-prone" person can stamp acute dysfunction on an organization. That person can shape his tongue as a weapon, shooting verbal bullets. Or he may plot schemes to harm the less politically dexterous. If thoroughly disaffected, he might just point a weapon at coworkers. He can have hundreds of targets if the organization does not have core values, policies and programs to help conflict prone individuals.

Where hard conflict is concerned, terms are often used differently. In this book, undermining can be achieved by a manager or non-managerial employee. In other words, anyone can undermine another person's respect and influence. Undermining happens behind the target's back, often when perpetrators are overtly friendly to the target. In this book bullying is defined as emotional and verbal abuse that is openly directed to an individual: face to face, no hiding. Bullying is separated from acts of violence for purposes of clarity, and the term violence in this book generally refers to physical attacks on people or property.

These three forms of hard conflict are interrelated – bullying thrives alongside undermining and serious cases of bullying are often the prelude to physical violence. The terms will now be explained further.

Undermining

Undermining is a form of political behavior that seeks to slowly strip away the target's influence or respect within the work setting. Undermining typically involves the strategic layering of truth with untruth about something the target has said or done when he is not present to defend himself. But there are misconceptions about undermining. Those genuinely trying to correct problems at work may be accused of undermining. Undermining is also contextual because even if we exaggerate someone's mistakes, this could be a function of misunderstanding more than malice.

Notably, there is a different standard in the national political context. Exaggerating the mistakes of a rival and downplaying his achievements behind his back is considered political dexterity, not undermining. Indeed, political acumen can also have a useful function in the workplace, edging out persons unfit for the positions they occupy. Astute organizational politicians can do a better job than those they edge out – much like the situation in national politics.

Clever undermining is virtually unreportable, since it is constituted of hearsay, negative rumor, innuendo or testaments from third party references. Undermining can only be prevented or managed by open communication channels, and this requires a culture cleanse, discussed in detail in Chapter 2.

There are two distinguishable schools of undermining. The first is undermining by not telling the truth. The second is undermining by telling the truth that has nothing to do with the person's character or performance.

Undermining By Not Telling The Truth

A good reason for telling the truth is to earn trust - if we catch a colleague in a major lie, trust plummets. But the complexity of lying needs to be explored here. When we talk about not telling the truth, a typical response is "well, everybody lies sometimes", or that no one hires a negotiator who tells the truth about everything. In the real world, no one thrives by telling the full truth about every single thing. Untruths range from the compassionate to the unkind, as suggested by Paul Eckman:

Lying is such a central characteristic of life that a better understanding of it is relevant to almost all human affairs. Some might shudder at that statement, because they view lying as reprehensible. I do not share that view. It is too simple to hold that no one in any relationship must ever lie; nor would I prescribe that every lie be unmasked. Advice columnist Ann Landers has a point when she advises her readers that truth can be used as a bludgeon, cruelly inflicting pain. Lies can be cruel too, but all lies aren't. Some lies, many fewer than liars will claim, are altruistic. Some social relationships are enjoyed because of the myths they preserve. But no liar should presume too easily that a victim desires to be misled.[4]

We are kinder to ourselves when we lie, but judge others. It is useful to know the absolutist-relativist distinction. Basically, when we judge others we tend to be absolutists, we are sure they are doing wrong as a result of their defective characters. When we deviate, we tend to attribute that deviation to the circumstances: I am a good person but the circumstances made me deviate. The absolutist-relativist distinction leads to a tornado of rationalizations, half truths and mixed messages in organizations with poor communication channels. According to Tom Peters, the mixed message environment in organizations has been known as "asking for A while rewarding B."[5]

Even listeners who are neutral toward a person may believe negative information about him because of the way it has been presented. Lay people are typically not very good at detecting either benign or malignant lies. Experimental research has revealed that the accuracy rate for detecting a lie ranges between 45% and 60%, when a 50% accuracy rate could be expected by chance alone. Most professional lie catchers, such as police officers, on average detect 54% of the truths and 49% of the lies.[6] Though highly observant persons are better at spotting liars, there is no proven way for a person to read another's mind.[7]

A manager or non-managerial employee tells lies about a colleague because the colleague has hurt him in some way, or is an impediment to the achievement of a particular goal. Not surprisingly, I have never found anyone openly admitting to undermining anyone in the present tense. If an individual trusts a coach, there might be some acknowledgement that she made things difficult for a colleague when the colleague did something wrong to her, a quid pro quo. If we look below at worst-case examples of undermining by not telling the truth, it would be difficult for anyone to admit to any of them:

1. Not giving the target the necessary information to do a job properly and then telling one's colleagues that the job has not been done properly.

2. Deliberately not checking out the accuracy of information, and then advising colleagues that the target should be denied a promotion based on that lapse.

3. Engineering a good candidate out of a promotion because she has not consented to having sexual relations: this is usually done by stressing or manufacturing the target's weak performance points to colleagues.

4. Arranging matters so that someone is late with a report, and then telling colleagues that the person gave in a late report.

5. Saying to a target that her idea is not workable and then bringing it up in a meeting as one's own idea, especially not in the hearing of the target.

6. In the absence of the target, taking full credit for another's significant work in terms of actually creating the work.

7. Telling the truth in such a manner as to discredit a person when that fact has nothing to do with the person's honesty or level of work.

8. Knowingly spreading false or partially false information to hurt a target.

Extending number 8, much of this information gets back to the target but is now hearsay or dependent on the testimony of persons who may not want to be involved in a dispute. People who undermine in this fashion have observed that other users of similar tactics have achieved major goals and are admired - only some have been "caught". Fortunately, people use undermining as a goal-achieving strategy far less when work stressors of a certain nature no longer exist.

Here's a case of undermining. 'John' blended truths, half truths, and manufactured evidence to report on the performance of the technicians who worked for him. John's boss, 'Richard', refused to believe him, even when the technicians were clearly wrong, because John had once manufactured evidence to have Richard fired, so that he could be promoted into his position. Richard was civil to John to protect his amicable working relationship with another executive, a strong ally of John. John left on his own after Richard continued to block his progress in ways such as holding up his application for a company car for over a year, using a variety of creative rationalizations for doing so.

The Human Resource Manager was surprised that the attitudes of the technicians did not automatically improve when working with John's replacement, who was clearly not a scheming sort. She did not realize that the technicians were so habituated to an undermining environment that they did not know how else to function. [8] The new manager eventually had to build a new team almost from scratch to get the work done properly.

And here we need to remember the emotional stain that undermining leaves on the undermined. Underminers can *embrace* the stain - as a man said in my hearing, "goody two shoes people get **** in this place!" To this point, once I had produced an original training policy for a company, which another person, 'Maude', claimed to have developed a couple of years later. What was interesting was that Maude had said of her former boss "she stole my documents and put her name on it, I cried myself to sleep at nights, when I realized what she had done." The former boss fell gravely ill and left the organization. Maude, the former victim, who now claimed that she had written the training policy, had perhaps learned that the person who had taken *her* work had thrived in the organization before becoming ill. This kind of situation is unfortunately not uncommon in organizations where the ethical fabric has been thinned.

Layering Truths With Untruths

Telling the truth to harm someone is classified as undermining if that "truth" has nothing to do with how the person works and serves to discredit her. This of course is different from mendacious undermining. There are heated debates about its ethicality because "truthful undermining" does not involve slander or libel.

"Truthful undermining" is using the truth to distort a listener's perception of a greater truth. The truth may be that the employee's father is in prison. Stating the truth is not undermining, it is how it is expressed: for example, inferring or stating openly "her father is in prison (fact) - this is the family she comes out of, and the apple does not fall very far from the tree." (inference) Having a parent in prison is of course rarely representative of how someone will perform in the workplace. In fact, because she has an incarcerated parent, she might go out of her way to be more straightforward in her dealings than her accusers. I was recently acquainted with a case where the faults of a woman were exaggerated by some of her peers almost immediately after it was discovered that her husband was in serious financial difficulties. She suddenly found herself undermined in an organization in which she had formerly been given special protection, by virtue of her husband's former position.

It is idealistic to state that there is any way to prevent undermining in organizations, especially in large or medium sized ones. The goal would be to significantly reduce its thickness and oiliness.

CHAPTER 1

Bullying

Bullying is not only seen in "bad" companies nor in companies that have below standard products or services. Like undermining, bullying is not only evident in "bad" people. An executive may be brutal to those who get in the way of his or the organization's goals, but be kind and even gentle otherwise. Little pleasure is taken in the aggression itself, it is simply a means to an end.

David Berreby reminds us that throughout history, young men who have been polite and kind to members of their own sort, who loved their parents and cared for their children, set out to kill other people's mothers and fathers and children without a qualm.[9] The same principle applies to bullying in the workplace. People can act differently in different settings.

Not only do many bullies have excellent qualities otherwise and almost always appear like normal people doing the things normal people do, but a lot of people called bullies are not. Shouting once or twice and being snappish may not be the best of traits, but it is wrong to label anyone doing this a bully. Very likely everyone has "bullied" in this manner during their lifetime. Real bullying, the regular, deliberate and often enjoyable bashing of another individual, is a hard-core conflict problem.

In so many of the cases I have witnessed, bullies have been asked to leave not because of the bullying itself but because their sense of power and entitlement led them to commit other infractions which could not be tolerated. In one case, an executive had been so accustomed to getting away with virtually every form of bullying, that he started to believe himself invincible, to the point where he stored his living room contents in one of the company's warehouses instead of paying for storage like a regular Joe. He was fired, to his great shock. Interestingly, an anti-bullying program helps to protect the bully! The habit of bullying usually starts in school. Some experts in the area have recommended that children should be taught to feel sorry for bullies, because they are unhappy, dysfunctional persons. Many bully-prevention school programs do not condemn the bully but instead help them to feel liked at school. [10]

Workplace bullying is often associated with a temper tantrum or a man persistently asking a colleague to do interesting things in bed with him. It's much more than that. Bullying constitutes a variety of punishments ranging from the mild to the severe, the common to the creative. Though bullying is normally associated with a series of behaviors, there are cases where one serious case of gratuituous aggression would merit the term "bullying".

Bullying, unlike undermining, is in-your-face, however subtly. Bullying can fit snugly in underlying and inferential behavior. Dismissive gestures are a substitute for shouting. A manager speaking to a junior manager in condescending tones can be more annoying than if she shouted at him only once. Words can be used in interesting ways. A Human Resource Manager told me she was continually referred to as a "resource" by an executive instead of as a "person" as the favored managers were called. She deliberately reduced her effectiveness, and undermined the executive who called her a resource. This is a classic example of the target morphing into a perpetrator.

Where companies are concerned, "bad" conveys different meanings. Four letter words may be accepted as a colorful outlet for anger and creativity in one company, in another it is a flagrant breach of company policy. What is *perceived* as wrong by the majority of employees affects their attitude. Bullying is sometimes confused with sternness and assertiveness, but it is quite different as these examples show:

- Threatening the target with physical violence, loss of job or poor performance reviews.

- Using abusive language to the target, especially when such language is not a cultural feature in that organization.

- Using a louder tone of voice toward the target than normally used to other colleagues.

- Making unwanted and unpleasant remarks (often couching them in humor) to a colleague about his race, religion, political affiliation, family, age, physical characteristics etc.

- Being generally abusive to, or very dismissive of, a colleague because of his or her unwillingness to consent to sexual relations.

- Arranging matters so that someone is late with a report, then blaming the target to her face for giving in a late report.

- Deliberately giving the target so much work that it cannot be done properly, then blaming the target to his face when the work is not done.

Doing the above in front of the targets' colleagues is an intensified form of bullying. The benchmark for bullying in the workplace is what would upset a person of ordinary sensitivity. To the over-sensitive, everything a person they dislike does will constitute bullying. By making frivolous complaints, they encourage others to be distrustful of those who have genuine cases.

It's difficult to bully, be a poor performer and be disliked by everyone. Persons who regularly bully usually have good work traits. In a nutshell, their actions are about control, fear, envy, and just not knowing how to act differently. Many persons who *appear* to be perpetrators don't even consider what they're doing to be "bullying", not knowing how else to conduct themselves in trying situations. Many say they're targets. I've heard "yes, I shout, but this is the fourth time I'm reminding her to read over her work, and that error in the salary calculation could have got me into real trouble with my boss." Or "yes, I said something to him, but look how he embarrassed me." Their response to this kind of aggravation is simply retaliation in their view.

My experience tells me that regular bullying is carried out by persons who need to be seen as "tough", "warriors", "goddesses" or "having cojones". When asked to reflect on "real toughness", they might suggest that "warrior" in its truest sense may be truly seen in a child battling cancer, a family who have previously experienced a series of significant misfortunes now facing bankruptcy yet forging ahead, soldiers in active battle or the victims of war.

We may come to an understanding that warriors are not supervisors who bully the colleagues who report to them, that's too easy. But actually, people who want to be viewed as super-tough *and* angry do have a point where *perception* is concerned. Though angry people may be perceived as cold and disreputable by some, they are viewed as competent, strong, dominant and intelligent by others.[11] The organization needs to explain the message it wants and needs to send, through a variety of ways, as discussed in Part 2.

The saying "all bullies are cowards" is not always true, and in addition is so rarely understood as to have virtually no meaning in

12

organizations where gratuitous aggression is a cultural feature. There is the bullying supervisor who will threaten his own manager. There is the low-self esteem bully, getting back at a target not because he shredded her original documents but because he does not smile enough at her: she will block the word "coward" from her emotional repertoire, and think "I am putting this person in his place."

There are of course clear cases where bullies are cowards. I have both heard of, and witnessed, abusers crying for their jobs in an executive's office, instead of handling the issue with contrition and grace. These persons assume markedly different personas: very respectful to colleagues with greater position status, bragging about the number of persons they have "put in their place" to peers or reportees, and then begging to keep a job. The image is not a comfortable one.

People can bully because of misconceptions, as seen in this example. A perpetrator, 'Peter', shared a not uncommon story. Peter's friend, 'Mike', had a teacher who repeatedly called him a dunce. Mike utilized the words "not dunce" as raw energy to rise in business. In fact, like the end of a good movie, Mike returned to that teacher "who had never even reached a vice principal" for the purpose of laying his successes on a gold platter before her. She had actually not remembered him (probably having told a lot of children they were stupid), but Mike reminded her of her comments issued a couple of decades ago. The surprised expression on her face was one of the most glorious moments in his life.

Peter felt that all adults *should* find the inward resources to "prove" to the person who has harmed them that they had made it big time in life. Through examination of the issue, however, Peter and I came to agree that the majority of persons might derive no benefits to being verbally abused and might even create a vicious cycle for themselves and others. We discussed the relationship between abused children, crime and drug use. Peter certainly did not want a teacher to call his own son a dunce. He even went further, saying that "staying a teacher" was not "so bad", since his favorite teacher had never been promoted to vice principal either.

Now Peter had bullied someone who reported to him. But it's not just the junior clerk whose emotions are battered by seniors - executives have reported of how other executives have traumatized them and that their employees aren't angels either. Bullied executives usually try to keep the harassment secret from others to deflect being viewed as weak. Where the general employee population is concerned however, a study has found that 96% of coworkers are aware of the bullying of another coworker.[12] But not all bullying is witnessed by anyone other than the perpetrator and target. Perpetrators may be adept at choosing their targets and planning their timing, and may use the subtleties of language and tone to make gratuitously unpleasant statements that are not easily re-expressed by the target, especially if the target is not particularly articulate – an awkward, bumbling interpretation of the meaning of somebody's body language only serves to make the target look impotent.

Bullying will affect other employees especially if they empathize with the target. But we tend to speak more about how bullying affects a target and coworkers rather than the perpetrator. Bully-ing affects perpetrators if their mistreatment of others bothers them in some way. Blended with the self indulgent thinking of "how I put that bastard in his place!" may be the underpinnings of guilt. Even if the bullying itself doesn't prick their conscience, they might worry about being exposed one day. They might appear to treat business as a game only, but perpetrators are as complex as anyone else - they need the admiration of others, and genuinely appear hurt when that admiration dries up. Perpetrators are also vulnerable in that they may become targets. Studies have estimated that approximately six out of ten targets plan revenge, and that revenge ranges from not following an instruction to calling the boss's wife to expose an extramarital affair.[13]

Bullying, Aggression and Incivility

Bullying is a form of aggression, but not all aggression is bullying. Focused aggression may be required to get ahead in many organizations. The aggression may be forgotten by everyone except the targets if the person ends up doing something good for the organizational or external community.

Richard Conniff gives the story of a manager who was pleasant and avoided controversy:

"Because he loathed office politics, he never bothered to appoint some scrappy lieutenant to fight on his division's behalf. The company was moving to new quarters. Other divisions, where the managers had a keener focus on rank and privilege, ended up with fewer cubicles and more real offices. They got doors! They got windows! The placid manager's division meanwhile got partitions. In fact, his demoralized employees were obliged to inventory their existing furniture so that the other divisions could cherry-pick the best stuff for their new offices. Sometimes, though we may not like to think it, it is better to live under a difficult, demanding alpha."[14]

A "difficult, demanding alpha" uses incivility as a tactic at appropriate times, but may in fact know all the ps and qs of the expected civilities. It is often difficult to draw the line between ignorance of civility and intentional incivility. Depending on the circumstances, one might give the uncivil colleague the benefit of the doubt.

Such as the case of 'Hilda' and her colleague, 'Millie'. Hilda criticized Millie's relative while Millie was seated at the same lunch table. Millie objected in low tones, and left the table quietly. Hilda was hurt. She had done nothing wrong and should be free to make comments about people reported in the newspaper as she saw fit, and no one should embarrass her by leaving the table. She phoned several colleagues to complain about Millie. When asked why she chose that method to express her anger, her reply was defensive "Why am *I* being singled out?" and suggested that it was always the "little man" who was always picked on. But when asked what her department stood for, she said "we are polite and nice to each other", and that she actually liked Millie, she had just forgotten that she was at the table. She certainly had not meant to be impolite.

The Baltimore Workplace Civility Study,[15] using a random sample of 400 employees from four Baltimore industries, found that over 40% of respondents had been victims of incivility two to four times in a month, and 25% had been in the victim role between five and ten times. Some of the behaviors the respondents considered to be uncivil were: refusing to work hard on a team effort project (90%), shifting the blame for your mistake to a coworker (88%), and reading someone else's mail (88%).

The researchers for the Baltimore Incivility Project[16] consider it unfortunate that workplace interventions generally accord little attention to civility. Incivility can have a significant negative impact in a department or even an entire organization. Incivility is usually a mix of ignorance and disrespect, and can be the precursor to violence.

The cost of workplace violence in Britain in 2001 may have been in excess of £30 billion.[17]

In the United States, 44% say they've worked for an abusive boss, according to a 2007 poll conducted by the Employment Law Alliance.

The UK Department of Health has assessed that between five and six million working days are lost each year to workplace stress and its effects.[18]

Violence

Recent research highlights the social implications of violence. Violent responses tend to become contagious in workplaces. Anderson and Pearson call attention to a phenomenon they refer to as "downward incivility spirals", whereby violence tends to be the result of patterns of escalating negative interactions between individuals in the workplace. For example, what begins as two individuals exchanging rude comments could eventually escalate into physical violence.[19]

Research suggests that the stress incurred from physical violence in the workplace is strongly associated with high turnover, reduced productivity, and lower employee commitment. Physical violence, which includes every kind of physical assault in addition to willful destruction of property, has been described as ugly, unnecessary, useful, sexy, and so on. Violence toward others, especially others not in one's own social group, has been condoned both openly and silently since the beginning of time. Violence is also viewed as strength, and for this reason there are those who are more attracted to perpetrators than to victims.[20]

Physical violence is rarely seen in offices decked with paintings and plants in which people are outfitted in business attire. Violence rendering bodily harm most likely erupts where large numbers of low remunerated workers toil under poorly supervised situations. Unless the organization is completely toxic or procedure-less, persons who initiate the violence are fired summarily. The violence impacts witnesses, namely secondary victims,[21] who have seen a sudden violent episode, and are still expected to work a few hours later or within the same week without any form of therapeutic intervention.

The Bureau of Labor Statistics' Census of Fatal Occupational Injuries reported that over 13,309 persons were killed in the workplace between 1992 and 2009.[22] The majority of those workers were probably assaulted in urban areas, and it is probable that any city in the world with a crime problem will have problems with violence in the workplace.

Physically violent acts deliver a particularly hard thump on organizational morale. Employees of all income levels initiate violence, but being physically violent at work is often ascribed to having a financially disadvantaged background or a background plagued with physical or emotional abuse - the latter term being increasingly correlated with being *over-indulged* as a child.

People will say "But I grew up in a violent, abused or over-indulged background and I'm not a bully or a criminal." They constitute the majority. Though being abused as a child will bring about an increased chance of becoming violent, 70% of abused children do not repeat their parents' violence towards them.[23] Individuals are more likely to be verbally or physically violent if they score highly on both narcissism and self-esteem.

What we do know is that the average person is not violent at work or at home. We also know that brain imaging surveys and other experiments show that being abused in the early years can damage the brain's function and structure, though whether this damage is permanent or not is moot. Electroencephalograms (ECGs), have accorded scientists the opportunity to observe brain wave abnormalities in 54% of adults who had undergone childhood abuse compared in only 27% of adults without early childhood trauma.[24] Also, abused children with a gene responsible for low levels of monoamine oxidase in the brain were nine times more likely to engage in violent or other antisocial behavior than persons with the same gene who were not mistreated.[25]

Violence can be interpreted as an act of shame, the shame of not knowing how to be a good student, spouse or employee. Other people, wittingly or unwittingly, can make us feel embarrassed about who we are or what we represent – and shame predisposes some of us to physical violence. James Gilligan discusses the shame ethic in society:

Another way to understand why shame motivates anger and violence toward others… is to remember that in a shame ethic, the worst evil is shame, the source of which is perceived as other people (the audience in whose "evil eyes" one is shamed). Therefore evil resides in other people, and to the degree that one feels shame, it is other people who deserve punishment. Punishing others alleviates feelings of shame because it replaces the image of oneself as a weak, passive, helpless, and therefore shameful victim of their punishment (i.e.) their shaming with the contrasting image of oneself as powerful, active, self-reliant, and therefore admirable, and unshameable…[26]

The author's observation is true for virtually all violent persons. It is worth noting however, that although shame may be a precursor to violence, violent sociopaths are often very charming and do not encumber themselves with shame or remorse.

Violence is sudden. 'Jonathon' hit a colleague 'Marvin' who asked for chicken at the canteen when none was available. Jonathon's reason for hitting Marvin was "he always asks for things that aren't there and gets on my nerves." His colleagues explained that there was more to the issue than food. Marvin's weak playing in the company football match purportedly resulted in a bad loss. Jonathon was livid. In conversation with Jonathon, I discovered that violence was a habit with him, that he had little else to be "proud" of. Major life themes were dissatisfaction with his job, a son in prison and another child failing in school. But the thought of his team winning a soccer match swelled his chest with pride, and here was this impertinent young man taking that rare pride away from him without a glimmer of remorse. To top it all, he then had the nerve to blatantly demand fried chicken in Jonathon's hearing. Jonathon had never learned how to manage disappointment, a critical life-skill.

Physical violence does not usually occur in a vacuum.[27] Examples of behaviors that might lead to physical violence are:

- Bullying, threatening coworkers either directly or indirectly.

- Boasting about aggressive behavior.

- Frequent conflicts with customers and colleagues.

- Bringing a weapon into the workplace when it is not a part of the job.

- Fascination with guns, weapons, statements which suggest that violence is the best way to address a problem.

- Discussions indicating despair over finances , home or work problems, belligerence, admiration of persons because of their violence, substance abuse, notable extreme change of behavior.[28]

If employees are not trained to observe these signs, they will gossip about their disaffected or strange colleague, proceed with their regular duties and be shocked when the colleague brandishes a weapon.

A brave social worker asked a young gunman how he would feel as a person without being armed with a gun or other form of weapon. The gunman became visibly upset just thinking about the question. His boyhood had apparently been simply a miserable chunk of time, and it was clear that he thought he was nobody and a target without his gun. In the context of the work place, we wonder if the violent person would deem himself a nobody and a target without engaging in the abuse. This young man was counseled by someone who could help him make sense of his emotions, and explain to him how he could change. If managers, supervisors and informal leaders really want to change their organizational culture, they can. In the vein of possibility, the following chapter looks at culture modification.

CHAPTER 2

Cleaning the Culture

We have an incomplete understanding of why hard conflicts exist, and know that physical violent acts are especially complex to understand and can even erupt in healthy organizations. We also know that there is less likelihood of violence, bullying and undermining existing in healthy workplaces.

Conflict is not addressed appropriately without a light, moderate or deep cleaning of the culture. Undermining, because of its more hidden nature, *cannot* be properly addressed without cleaning the enterprise's clogs and blockages, regardless of the conflict management system employed. Fortunately, the cleaning improves all major functions of the organization – from production to marketing to finance. Work life of course does not become perfect after the cleaning, but assuredly more habitable.

Cultures and Conflict

There are surface and deep aspects to a culture in as much as there are surface and deep aspects to conflicts. The surface culture is immediately noticeable and visible, for example, the way employees greet each other and the procedure they use to file their documents. The deep culture is the set of spoken and unspoken beliefs, rules, customs, knowledge and norms which define how the particular organization operates. The deep culture can serve to prevent employees from admitting that serious disharmony exists, if the image of a healthy functional organization must be protected at all costs.

Disharmony resonates in negative politics, such as keeping friends close, and enemies closer to harm or outwit them. Leaders may not be aware of the variety of phenomena that represent deep conflict, such as the continual spreading of negative rumors target-ing groups based on their status, ethnic origin and so on. Strikes and similar actions mean that the substantive issues leading to the disruption have spawned increasing levels of anger for a relatively long period. Increased theft is not necessarily viewed as unethical in the circumstances and notably, only one in 35 employees is ever apprehended for theft[29] in the United States. That figure would be similar or higher in most other countries.

Cultures plagued with undermining and bullying do work, in that they make monetary profits. Yet there are costs when employees' emotions are steeped daily in a noxious atmosphere – significant net profits may exist, just not anywhere as much as there could be. Not everyone is unhappy in conflict laden cultures either: intrinsically motivated persons may work well despite high levels of disharmony. Some persons have philosophies that essentially mean: "the workplace doesn't have to be paradise, it's only where I work." Others may look more directly at benefits: "there are people problems, but there are some really good people here and I get a good salary." Though these are salubrious attitudes, they ironically serve to keep the organization in ill-health.

The Need for a Conceptualizing Manager

An effective conflict prevention program is a fully integrated array of philosophies, values, strategies and tactics that interact and integrate with each other. This program is initiated by at least one conceptualizing manager (CM). The CM is the town crier with successful communication skills who fully understands that the level of distrust in the organization has reached a point where it impacts the well being of himself and his colleagues, and impairs the future of the organization.

The CM is not usually the CEO if the CEO is not in the rough and tumble of daily operational matters. The CM is usually the most senior Human Resource Officer (HRO) or someone with authority and influence to advise the chief that something is going wrong and let's do something about it. However, if a potential CM feels that her heralding will be greeted by hostility or that all of the work for culture modification will be heaped upon her, she will be of two minds whether to initiate the program or not – especially if such work is not explicitly stated on her terms of reference.

STAGE 1: RESEARCH

The research done by the CM is not as extensive as the one conducted by a formal change-agent, it is simply enough to issue the first warning. The CM initiates the ground work phase by observing the departments that have natural conflict with each other, such as a production department and sales department. He asks:

1. How are the members of those departments getting along?

2. What time of year is conflict at its best or worst, or does the level of conflict tend to be consistent?

3. Are there healthy doses of creative tension, or has creativity descended into intractability? Are the members really interested in having the conflicts resolved?

4. Is it only these two departments that are walled in by conflict, or the entire organization?

5. Does the conflict take the form of undermining, bullying or both?

6. Has there been a recent case of physical violence among the employees?

7. Does the organization or department have a laissez-faire culture,[30] often seen in monopolies or those companies on a downward spiral? [31]

8. Do influential employees appear to accept the high level of conflict, believing it to be the oil that smoothes the path to challenging goals?

9. Can the conflicts be resolved or improved?

Where the last question is concerned, "improvement" means that residual difficulties exist but that the persons wrapped up in previous conflicts work well together - this is perhaps the most realistic scenario in the majority of cases.

The CM of course also needs to present hard information to the CEO and other colleagues on energy robbers. Examples of energy-robbers are decreasing revenue, business cancellations, valued customers leaving to go elsewhere, increased employee grievances, sick leave days and violent incidents. Interestingly, I heard a CM refer to energy-robbers as energy-terrorists to get the attention of his colleagues.

The Presentation

Good CMs see in black and white when necessary, in several shades of black when required, and will usually have an idea about the right approach based on the culture. He will know whether to speak to the CEO alone first, do a short PowerPoint presentation about interpersonal dynamics and their relationship with productivity with his peers, or another strategy. Most importantly, the CM presents his concerns in an unthreatening manner so that every-one sees that he is not indulging in a finger-pointing exercise. I would also avoid giving any kind of complicated map or route to organizational health at this time, which may be as confusing as it is impressive-looking: some, including very good leaders, may only see a system full of distended veins and will not necessarily admit to not understanding it in the presence of their peers.

The CM should be careful about suggesting that the entire culture should be changed – culture is modified more than changed, and there would be valuable features of the culture which kept that organization in survival mode.

A good dose of wisdom is required. I knew a manager who had read an article about the necessity of finding out who benefits from any unpleasant situation, and actually asked his peers "we have to ask ourselves - who is benefitting from this (problem) in this company?" Not surprisingly, his colleagues felt he was accusing them of underhand actions. Tact and discernment are required – when leaders say "we tell it like it is here", that statement does not invite a carte blanche for candidness – you still need to know *how* to tell it like it is.

A positive, enthusiastic presentation will not work in many cultures. It is likely that listeners, especially those over thirty-five years of age, will know of new ventures that someone was really enthusiastic about and yet did not work. Even excellent systems like the Balanced Scorecard are rendered impotent and ridiculous under the heavy weight of protracted disharmony. It is useful to remember that one's colleagues will not necessarily embrace change[32], even if it is positive, seeing it as more work to be heaped upon their already weighty terms of reference.

I recommend a positive-neutral approach. I advise the CM to keep the essentials to phrases such as "I think we are being hurt and we don't have to be hurt", "we need to change the way people learn around here and what we give them to learn", "with appropriate change we have X percentage of market share again" and similarly pithy statements expressed in a culturally appropriate mode. He should speak as directly and simply as possible, and avoid the current management and technical jargon unless everyone there fully understands what is being said.[33]

The CM makes a decision at this point, largely based on the reactions of his colleagues. If he is given a road, however narrow, on which to proceed, he might want to suggest that a change agent be engaged, whether internal or external. Or he may wish to continue his presentation at a later date, or ask if others might want to join him in making the presentation. Indeed, the CM must be politically astute enough to influence those persons who are naturally proactive and who really want the organization to prosper. The questions below will guide the CM to actions which indicate proactive and reactive stances to conflict management. He should of course use his own language and style.

- Is there a deliberate attempt to evaluate the effectiveness of communication/trust/conflict in this company?

  Yes   **No –**

           What are the possible consequences?

- Are alternative management/organizational practices compared and evaluated for their ability to generate creative or destructive conflict?

  Yes   **No –**

           What are the possible consequences?

- Are any changes in the system deliberately designed to improve conflict?

  Yes   **No –**

  What are the possible consequences?

- Has there been a realistic plan on how the conflict management system will be maintained and evaluated?

  Yes   **No –**

  What are the possible consequences?

If a CM does not want to directly discuss conflicts, he could ask: do we have deliberate strategies to retain our talented individuals – are you *more inclined* to say a yes or a no? Are we enabling enough creativity and innovation – yes or no? Are we strongly encouraging effective communication practices – yes or no? The CM may ask his peers to pose any yes/no questions they want answered. Any "no" answer indicates a conflict of some nature. The CM will also appear much more credible – and more human and likeable - if she also admits that she or her department is not all perfect. There exists a good dose of cynicism in the hearts of colleagues who are obliged to listen to prolonged "preaching" delivered by the imperfect, though many, in view of maintaining the peace, may maintain professional facial expressions. It is this silent cynicism that wrecks many an initiative that could lead to great outcomes.

Now what the credible CM has achieved is the promotion of a liberating discomfort, not dangerous comfort. The liberating discomfort suggests that most if not all of the leaders are recognizing that the emperor (the culture) is busily taking off his clothes in public. Someone might say "let's focus on our strengths instead." For change to be sustainable, there should be a focus on both strengths and weaknesses.[34] Keith Hammonds suggests that Highly Reliable Organizations (HROs) do not let their successes harm them, and cautions:[35]

> "Don't be tricked by your success. HROs don't gloat over their successes. In fact, it's just the opposite: They are pre-occupied with their failures. They are incredibly sensitive to their own lapses and errors, which serve as windows into their system's vulnerability. They pick up on small deviations. And they react early and quickly to anything that doesn't fit with their expectations... HROs create climates where people feel safe trusting their leaders. They question assumptions and report problems. They quickly review unexpected events, no matter how inconsequential. They encourage members to be wary of success, suspicious of quiet periods, and concerned about stability and lack of variety, both of which can lead to carelessness and errors."

The CM expects resistance and plans for same. For example, a colleague could say – "listen, this organization has won awards, could there be that much of a problem?" The colleague might not be aware that winning awards is only one aspect of health: some of the companies that experienced serious financial challenges on Wall Street in 2008 had recently received awards. Companies are subject to the laws of gravity and it can even take ten years for an organization to slowly disintegrate because one of two vibrant departments deflect a rapid fall.

Having the Energy and Financial Resources to go through the Process

If the CM has received the enthusiastic go-ahead of the CEO, the culture cleanse will likely reduce the degree of congestion. The CM and her colleagues also need to assess if the organization has the energy and financial resources to go through a major change process. The most sustainable change is one step at a time. In large organizations, change is best started – and tested – in a specific department or unit.

Managers and supervisors are the real executors of highly challenging plans, not formal change-agents, and it takes "stress energy" to substantially change any large or medium sized organization. So even when the managers are very loyal to the company, but lack physical and psychic energy, they slow down the formal change agents or make their work minimally effective.

A manager told me "anybody can see this place needs change, but I don't want them to lump it on me, I'm tired." Fatigue had led him to chronic cynicism regarding the utility of new systems. A practical idealist, he had never believed that culture change in a large organization could occur seamlessly, and had bolstered the organization into positive activity. But after the excitement and enjoyment of it eroded, and some unexpected problems occurred, the nitty gritty of single-execution took a toll on his health. Single-execution does not work for long: managers and supervisors collaboratively do the work to modify a culture. Protecting the health of key leaders requires a strategic plan in itself (also see Chapter 6). If the stakeholders are convinced that the change effort will result in benefits from them, they will be reenergized.

The Company's Energy

An audit on the collective energy of the team is a most useful exercise. A confidential questionnaire is used to ask the leaders or all employees how energetic and healthy they feel at work. A simple questionnaire is in order. For example, if only physical health is addressed, the questionnaire could be developed using a five point Likert scale – or need only contain three items (1) I feel very healthy most of the time (2) I feel healthy most of the time (3) I feel tired/sick most of the time. This makes for fascinating results. An internal or external expert might develop a questionnaire that also includes items on how respondents feel about the level of conflict in their departments, and statistical tools are used to correlate respondents' energy levels to their perception of the levels of conflict. The respondents may also be asked what kind of change would encourage them to be energetic, or happier with each other.

Changing the pale of a conflicted culture to the glow of health will help the company to achieve challenging goals with less effort – but of course this takes resources (or consumes resources for cash-strapped organizations). If an Ombudsman is needed, that's a salary, and if the most respected managers and other employees are invited to sit on a conflict resolution committee, opportunity costs are implied.

Resolving protracted conflicts do not only infer changing the organizational structure, but physical structures. For example, engineers would need to reconfigure the plant if the workers are in conflict with the manager about working in the heat, and that is why sometimes managers choose not to see conflicts when they either don't have the financial resources, or need or choose to spend it elsewhere. Though not ideal, reducing the conflict would suggest giving the persons working with heat the necessary suits, and drinks with which to replace the electrolytes, until the funds are available to restructure the factory. Though culture modification should ensure an increase in profits, a balance should be forged in less wealthy organizations (also see Chapter 7 – A Single Manager's Influence).

STAGE 2: WHEN THINGS START TO HAPPEN

The CM will likely be involved in the change effort. If the organization has fewer than 100 employees, the leaders could go the basic route of that given in the box on the following page, as long as some of the leaders are able project managers. But the initial change process can be even simpler. I know a CEO of a company of less than 80 persons, who gave his managers, supervisors and key non-supervisory staff a power talk replete with new information and reminders on Monday mornings. He is convinced that these personal talks had a substantial effect on the company's profitability.

He ensured that the required execution was done properly. There are many great programs out there – programs that look at systems, how to build trust and so forth. The justifications given for implementing these programs are extremely seductive – x and y company has done extremely well with this program, we show you how to instill trust, communicate better, align systems using this new model – and so forth. Yet the Blanchard report states that up to 70 percent of all change initiatives do not succeed because there is not a set strategy for *managing* the changes, and failed changes can lead to greater problems. The report also found, among other things, that companies need to have a unified voice about the change, and that effective change requires a unified approach from all persons who will have an effect on the change.[36] But once key persons really *want* the program succeed, that program will most likely succeed.

STEPS TOWARD HEALTH: AN EXAMPLE OF CULTURE CHANGE FOR REDUCING CONFLICT AT A SMALL ORGANIZATION (LESS THAN 100 PERSONS)

Create an exciting and meaningful vision: The organization's goal may not be to "reduce conflict" per se but to become an Organization of Choice, an award-winner, a medium sized or small company with the pride of being known for its high-quality services, or an organization which has a certificate from the employees stating that it is "the best company to work for", which in itself has implications for wonderful public relations.

Develop SMARTER[37] Goals: The focus should be on translating great intentions into actions and outcomes that are observable.

Use a variety of thinking skills: Examine ideas by using Edward deBono's Six Thinking Hats[38] or any other protocol that encourages many different kinds of thinking.

Establish a Central Coordinating Point – it's good to have an advisory group comprised of persons from several departments to monitor the entire process and be a link with everyone. At least one person in the group should be trained in project management.

Try out changes in small work groups first. Give the groups information on which behaviors are being demonstrated and which ones need to be improved.

Celebrate successes. Small successes merit x and any large successes merit X. This injection of enjoyment into the process is the best glue to ensure the maintenance of the new system.

Have constant and vigilant surveillance of the new inter-ventions.

If the company has sufficient financial resources, it should go the route of organization development (OD). There is no established typology for OD, which focuses on systems and task requirements. There are new technologies, strategies and methods associated with the field almost every year. OD may include a combination of any of the following: survey-feedback, establishing values and goals, various ways to encourage employees to adopt the organization's values and goals, setting up various kinds of measurements, changing the organization structure and design, promoting a learning organization, employing various kinds of trust building exercises between and among teams. Names for specific inter-ventions include root-cause analysis, the Balanced Scorecard, Total Quality Management models, International Standards Organization and so on.[39] Organization development experts are change-experts. Every successful manager is an OD expert in her own way, and if these resources can be tapped, OD specialists will have many more lasting success stories.

Trying to eradicate or temper bullying, undermining, or any other organizational problem quickly, will not work if the roots of tension are deep. For this reason, OD consultants tend to start with strategic change, the foundation for all other changes. The consultants know that external competition destroys or significantly harms organizations that fail to change when required. Departments become ineffective one at a time or simultaneously.

Because of the uncertain value of new strategies, strategic change is perceived to be beneficial for low-performing organizations and harmful for high-performing organizations. Strategic inertia there-fore exists in high-performing organizations, as major changes are required even in these enterprises with past successes.[40]

After the team of consultants and key stakeholders have agreed on the definition of the problem, the next step is the diagnosis or audit, which may actually lead to a different definition of the problem. A comprehensive full-culture audit is preferred, rather than audits of a particular department or system. Good auditing will allow for the future cleansing which removes the blockages from the flow of not only conflict resolution systems but of all systems. Organizations may have a loggerhead of systems – systems for customers, systems for staff in this area and so on that are not in tandem with each other, and so clog up each other. Systems can create distrust and confusion – sometimes just clearing up the systems will lead to better communication and trust.

There are various ways to audit a culture, and the number of steps involved could be 5 or 50, depending on the size, complexity, strengths and weaknesses of the culture. The change agents would know that no conflict is the same, as much as no organization is the same. They ask more detailed questions than the CM. They use comprehensive and validated questionnaires which are also very useful for pre-test and post-test purposes. The analysis of interviews, completed questionnaires and other research instruments will show strengths and opportunities for improvement.

Examples of questions that could be asked at the audit are given below. On the bright side, these are great questions for learning about the organization. On the flip side, such questions will either be difficult or time consuming for many organizational leaders to respond to and trained auditors would know how to introduce the questions – and if and when to use some of them.

1. Fundamentals

- What is the history of this company? (other than what is shown on the website)
- What fortunate and challenging occurrences happened during the past decade – and how do they affect the culture today?
- Are there any traditions that are helpful? Any that are counter-productive?
- What are the company values? How are the values being lived?
- What is the stated and actual mission and vision?
- What are the objectives and the progress made on those objectives over the last year/five years?

2. Performance (For the organization, departments and individuals)

- How is performance measured?
- What is done when performance is less than expected?
- What is done when performance is better than expected?

3. Knowledge

- What is the skill and knowledge set in this company?
- Why does this skill and knowledge set exist?
- Is knowledge managed strategically?[41]
- How are people taught?
- How do they learn?
- How is their learning followed up?

4. Operational Systems

- What are the financial and other operational systems?
- How well are they working? What are the successes and the blockages?

5. Communication

- What are the major elements in the communication system?
- What works and what does not work?
- How are decisions made?
- In whose interest are those decisions? (this is a tricky question – if the culture is charged with suspicion, delete it from the list of questions)
- How is work communicated?
- What can or should not be discussed?
- If there is open communication, what is meant by "open"?

6. Conflict (General)

- What are the costs of conflict to everyone? Can examples be given?
- How do people react to good news of others and how do they react to bad news?
- Generally speaking, do employees respond to changes with conflict, with acceptance or with creativity?
- How do conflicts end up – under the rug, explosive, dealt with ineffectively or effectively?
- What does the formal conflict management system look like?

7. Undermining, Bullying and Physical Violence

- How many employees would categorize this organization as highly political? Why?
- What is the level of civility? Generally good, poor, do you know how this came about?
- How many reports are there of bullying?
- How many threats of physical violence were there in the past five, two years or one year?[42]

Good OD consultants know that change is generally slow in large organizations, and do the following to ensure that interventions have a chance to work well.

1. Recommendations should have the full support of top management. Culture change is a change in values (see the following chapter). If top management has not bought into the new set of values, interventions will generally be a waste of time, money and energy.

2. There must be accountability for the deliverables, and the consequences for not achieving them should be outlined.

Nonetheless, real problems that are encountered in executing the promises must be taken into consideration.

3.   All the organization's people must be involved in each phase of cultural modification. This is challenging for many organizations because of the time it can take. The time is significantly shortened when everyone learns the guidelines for communicating with respect and clarity.

Culture modification needs to be accelerated where physical violence is concerned, and waiting to obtain everybody's buy-in on the required changes is counterproductive. If the organization has suffered from a violent incident, it is recommended that experts in the area of security be immediately engaged.

Violence of course incurs very heavy costs to employers. Costs include extending psychological care for victims and secondary victims, heightening security measures, and mending a battered public image. But even with heightened violence in many societies, most employees are unprepared to deal with violent episodes. The involvement of persons with diverse expertise and experience is especially critical due to the depth and complexity of physical violence prevention.

Of note, violence may surface in the workplace setting, outside of the workplace setting (two workers carrying a grudge from work, or a riot that leads itself into companies, especially those that sell or warehouse goods), and where domestic violence is brought into the workplace. These forms of violence require specific interventions.

The first step in a course of violence prevention is to assess the history of physical violence in that workplace and the risks and exposures. Some of the risk factors include exchanging money with the public, delivering goods, guarding possessions of significant value, working alone or in small groups, especially late at night or during early morning hours and carrying out inspections, and working in crime-prone areas. In addition, working with very angry individuals is a risk factor, often found in hospitals and criminal justice settings.

Risk assessment also includes the experience of other companies in the same business to ascertain if they have low or high levels of employee disgruntlement, and their proactive or reactive experiences in managing violence. In addition, risk assessment includes the conducting of cultural assessments to measure employees' attitudes and beliefs about physical violence. Individuals who express abusive anger frequently are maladjusted.

Though the typical risk assessment may not take into consideration attachment issues, a most important way to prevent workplace violence is indeed social, and this is where security experts work with organization development experts. A sound workplace violence prevention program ensures that all employees have an understanding and attachment to the company's core values and code of conduct, and therefore to each other, further discussed in the following chapter. Violent persons generally feel alone and vulnerable. Anger arising from frustrated attachment needs can lead to nonadaptive behavior aimed at receiving negative attention, often considered better than receiving no attention at all.[43]

Once a picture of likely problems has been constructed, the next step is evaluating existing controls. Specific expertise is required for areas such as employee selection and recruitment, cash control, exits and entry, lighting control, signage, training and the many areas associated with violence prevention. To prevent unnecessary frustration, disappointment, injustice and alienation, experts look at the design of work and work processes, while also empowering employees with the skills to act appropriately when their anger rises. A proactive collaboration with the local police is recommended.

The management of violent *acts* is yet another field of expertise. If the organization has been a victim of physical violence, management should ensure that key persons are given crisis management training specific to violent acts (see also Chapter 4). Managers, supervisors and nonsupervisory staff in the most vulnerable departments or areas would need to understand at least some aspects of surveillance and diversionary tactics, intervention modalities, physical restraint and isolation techniques. Each of these areas is a large study in and of itself.

Clearly, it is best if organizations, especially those located in violence-prone communities, employ executive or middle-management officers with experience in security, such as the police or the military. Violence prevention and management is particularly critical if the organization is burdened with a history of physical violence – a proactive stance can save lives, money and protect the organization's reputation. [44]

Emile Durkheim and Refreshment

It takes humility, wisdom and caution to change a culture. Humility to recognize when we don't know how to go about something. Wisdom to reflect while gathering as much information as we can on the subject.[45] The great sociologist, Emile Durkheim, made this statement:

"Just as our organism gets *refreshment* (italics mine) outside itself, so our mental organism feeds on ideas, sentiments, and practices that come from society."[46]

The organization can be transformed into an enterprise of refreshment. Though disaffected employees say "the workplace is no family, that's just PR" the workplace does have similarities to a family life – they are both groups of people dependent on each other for critical needs – fiscal, professional and to varying degrees – emotional. A study of inappropriate belligerence in adopted families compared the family environment developed by their biological families with that of their adopted families. When the children born into an aggressive environment were adopted by the more peaceful families, only 13% of the adopted children demonstrated anti-social behaviors they grew up with. When these children lived with families with a history of aggression, 45% of the children became violent.

It's not only children who thrive or are hindered by their environment. One's place of work is where one spends the most daylight hours during Monday to Friday – indeed, a second place of residence. Adults become more emotionally mature in a culture where they can develop and work well. Once the culture changes, bullying, negative politics, incivility, active discrimination and physical violence – all features of adolescent-type behavior – will either clear up or improve.

Virulent behavioral viruses must be purged for significant innovation to take place. Firms have been creative in their cleansing modes – for example, giving teams challenging goals that are impossible to achieve with the current technology, but which would also be very difficult to achieve with the kind of conflict that saps creativity. It was challenging goals that helped to realize Canon's disposable copier cartridge and Toyota's hybrid engine.[47]

Cultures rarely change significantly before two years unless bought out by another company and new management arrives armed with new agendas. Culture modification is crucial: in the United States, only 29% of employees report being engaged in their jobs and 16% are actively disengaged.[48] Organizational values are clearly not being shared or not viewed as credible.

The remainder of this book continues with the theme of culture change under different headings. In most organizations, the establishment of values is a powerful way to successfully modify the culture. I have enjoyed working for organizations which control conflict well without an announcement of core values, but large and medium sized organizations are served well with articulated core values.

CHAPTER 3

Values and the Integrated Conflict Management System

E very culture contains strong values, whether they are splashed on a billboard or in the psyche of the employees. Values give meaning to everything we do at work – positive values like "we will do the work of an ill colleague without complaint" to cautious values like "watch your back". Organizations often have stated core values, but the incongruity of lovely values with protracted disharmony means that disharmony will continue to be victorious.

Fairness is a particularly important core value. Studies have indicated that executives can gain agreement for their decisions by making those decisions in ways employees deem fair.[49] Fairness denotes respect, and when fairness is a shared value, there is reduced undermining and no bullying and physical violence.

Organizations with a common set of core values were able to succeed during trying times in the past. When no one knew how to respond to the new challenges, the sharing of common values helped companies make choices on which employees could agree.[50] Using this line of reasoning, the ability of the organization to survive through difficult times is compromised if there is limited understanding of the positive values required. Indeed, positive core values become the common language of the organization. The core values help employees solve dilemmas by providing them with answers to "what should I do?" when faced with challenges. The core values should be known and understood before or during the development of an integrated conflict management system.

Codes of Conduct

The best conflict management systems do not occur in a vacuum. The company's values should be developed or modified before or during the development of the integrated conflict management system. Positive values are shared in many ways – and one major way is through a relevant and widely understood Code of Conduct. This document helps to assure respect and therefore becomes a safeguard against undermining, bullying and physical violence.

A statement which attests to the need for guidelines are the Archbishop of Canterbury's statement to the House of Lords in Britain in 1994:

Since the right motivation is not enough by itself, all of us need guidelines and codes to help us realise (our) good intentions in practice. Such codes are vital for institutions as well as individuals, mobilising authority and peer pressure behind ethical norms and translating general values into specific expectations.[51][52]

The advantages of a Code of Conduct include the creation of a positive, law-abiding culture, the early detection of misconduct and the prevention of civil and criminal liability. But how does one proceed from one level of conduct to another level? I believe that there should first be a leadership Code of Conduct, which may be a separate document or the first chapter/section in the general code of conduct.

The Leadership Code of Conduct

Managers and other employees relate hundreds of cases where organizational leaders would have benefitted from a shared leadership code of conduct, developed by the leaders themselves. The code is not so detailed as to curtail the creativity of the managers, and includes at least one statement on how conflicts among leaders should be managed.

I recently shopped at a supermarket during a very busy period, and a long line waited on a single cashier, while the six other cashier stations remained vacant. I noted a well designed and particularly attractively framed code of customer care and team work over the store manager's booth. I politely asked the manager if he was able to put on an additional cashier, and he mumbled something incoherent without looking at me. I left it at that. Five minutes later he spoke sarcastically to the cashier in front of the customers, which he should not have even done behind our backs. The result?

He exposed customers to a surly cashier who muttered under her breath and seemed to be in a rush to discuss the manager with her peers.

The beautifully written Code with the vibrant colors had done little to produce pleasant attitudes, and there was nothing in the Code that spoke to the special responsibility that leaders have concerning interpersonal relationships. The Code's visibility and beauty might have led to further resentment, if clashing with a hidden and unattractive reality. When leaders feel something is deeply wrong in the organization, no Code professionalizes their behavior. This is why it is so important to start the process of changing the culture before developing a Code.

Conventional wisdom dictates that there will always be some clash between our ideals, represented in a Code, and what we actually do. Effective sensitization programs acquaint leaders with the skills to re-channel their energies on their individual and collective well-being, thereby engineering a much softer clash. Leaders would ideally meet at least once per year to discuss how they are coping with their Code – what's working, what's not working, and what needs to be done.

The Code for All the Organization's Citizens

Apart from discussing necessary issues like fraud and care of company property, the Code should address interpersonal issues, namely:

Commitment: To my success and safety and the success and safety of my department and everyone in the organization.

Communication: I do my part to communicate effectively and openly, listening keenly to others and expecting that they will listen keenly to me. I communicate in a nonviolent, emotionally intelligent [53] manner.

Progress: Since I want my company to help me achieve my life and professional goals, which includes my family and my community, I will help the organization to achieve its major goals.

We can see that if employees learn how to work with the values above, that conflict will usually not be protracted.

If no Code of Conduct previously existed, employees should play a role in deciding its contents. Experienced leaders know that value-based initiatives like Codes of Conduct have significant meaning only when managers and employees from various departments have participated in aspects of its development.

The development of the Code for the general employee population is a project and should therefore be developed in an organized fashion. The guidelines for the Code involves:

a) A description of project/program objectives and activities to be covered by the agreement.

b) Plans for the human and financial resources required for its completion.

c) A time-frame/plan of action for the implementation of the project.

d) An assessment of the capacity building required.

e) A description of responsibilities of the participants and whom they are accountable to.

f) Accountability in terms of time-frames for delivering progress reports and to whom.

g) Time-frames for evaluations, reviews and how modifications will be made and communicated.

h) A plan for the resolution of conflict over the Code – yes, it can produce conflicts!

Within this project frame, meetings are held with stakeholders who are often asked the one to three values that would be of most benefit to the enterprise's health. An internal specialist, consultant or legal officer prepares the first draft of the Code. The best Codes are user-friendly – employees can quote them when discussing standards of interpersonal behavior at work.

After the first draft of the Code of Conduct has been submitted, a representative sample of employees are asked about the most memorable points in the document, and why those points stand out to them. If the Company wanted their stance on good inter-personal relations to leap out at readers, but what the readers really got was a booklet full of multisyllabic words, the Code won't achieve very much. If employees have been involved at some level, they will more easily remember the three – or six – most important things about the Code.

Values must be defined in behavioral terms to make the valued behaviors observable and measurable. Teams should share how the values can work with each other. Members of the production team can be asked to discuss how "respect for self and others", stated as a value in a Code of Conduct, impacts both occupational safety and production targets. A Marketing Manager could give suggestions on the visual and verbal techniques that ensure the widest dissemination and attractiveness of campaigns for the

CEO to launch the Code of Conduct. A member of the Finance and Accounting team could highlight the need for good interpersonal relationships by providing a costing of a protracted conflict, taking into account all of the opportunity costs in a fictional unit. This level of participation makes the exercise hands-on rather than something the executives got up to.

It is astonishing what employees can come up with when inspired to do so, and would probably be more creative than the road that I have developed below:

Respect
Open communication
Accurate communication
Deep work performance

---

*THE **ROAD** TO **HEALTH** AND **PROFIT***

"Deep" work performance might raise a few eyebrows, and spark interest in a Code. The organization coins its own meaning for deep, dedicated or devoted performance, which of course has effective conflict management as one of its bases. That could mean performance which takes into consideration the needs of external customers, for example.

The Formal Conflict Management System

Once the Code of Conduct has been accepted by the majority, it is much easier to develop or improve the formal conflict management system. Successful integrated conflict management systems contain, at the very least, the following:

1.   A variety of conflict resolution options, which are rights based and interests based.[54]

2.   Ways to prevent and identify all kinds of conflicts, at all levels.

3.   The opportunity for users to readily identify and access support persons who are knowledgeable about the conflict management system.

4.   A focus on finding out the causes of conflicts and on problem solving.

5.   A general future-oriented approach: however, physical violence and the more serious instances of undermining and bullying requires an assessment of past actions.

Gleason argues compellingly that the characteristics of those who make the complaints should be considered when designing an integrated conflict management system, ensuring that support for the system exists throughout the entire infrastructure of the organization, saying:

> Those who speak up about conflict management design are not necessarily those who will find themselves suddenly in need of a complaint system. This is especially true in a multicultural context. Many people who speak up about dispute resolution have thought mainly about the interests of employers, the rights of complainants or respondents, organizational development principles, or conflict resolution

theory, all of which are important, and all of which contribute to the design of procedures people think complainants should want. But considering what complainants actually want, which is, if possible, to raise concerns *as they personally wish to raise them*, is critical to ensuring that a system is actually used." [55]

She continues to state that the most common characteristic of people who have a concern or grievance is that they just wish their problem would go away. Employees may have concerns about doing nothing, about taking action or feeling that they must take action. Other employees may want revenge, some may enjoy the fight, and some wish to disrupt the workplace.[56] Systems should provide support for these employees and others to find and use constructive options.

A conflict resolution system should be tailored accordingly to size, operations and general environment. Does the organization mostly have disputes? "Disputes" may be short-term conflicts and "conflicts" may represent longer term clashes with greater potential for intractability. Is there such a long history of conflicts of interests and values among the participants have resulted in the emergence of *behavioral conflict*, where the participants have, over the years, developed significant mistrust of each other?[57]

The conflict management system should be developed by representatives from the various layers in the organization, also taking into consideration the most common "users of the system" as recommended by Gleason. The system would apply to managers, supervisors, employers, clients, contractors and others who have a relationship with the organization. Very importantly, the system should ensure that no reprisals are made against reporting employees, unless mischief is clearly a factor.

Below is a step by step procedure for developing the integrated conflict management system. Like all procedures, many times one has to return to a previous stage to see if that was done thoroughly before proceeding. It is also important that skilled and knowledgeable persons, and operational and financial resources, be identified for each stage.

Stage 1: Define the problem

- Define what a conflict is (not everyone agrees on what constitutes a conflict).
- Identify the clogs in the organization – what is too slow, too complicated, too disorganized, not measured or just not working.
- Ascertain if the clogs were created because of conflicts, ignorance, or another factor.
- Determine if the organization's vision is affected by conflict.

Stage 2: Determine the steps that need to be taken to get the vision and the actuality into greater alignment by writing objectives

- Clarify the general and specific objectives of what is required, noting that these objectives may change as other questions are answered.
- Convert the objectives into steps.

Stage 3: Identify and diagnose the causes of major organizational conflicts

- Analyze the root causes of any gaps between the goal and the present reality.
- Determine the effectiveness of the existing conflict handling procedures.
- Identify the formal and informal leadership and other key participants and their roles in the conflicts.

Stage 4: Examine the range of options for additional procedures or revisions of existing procedures

- Identify Improvement Options.
- Assess the strengths and weaknesses of Improvement Options.

Stage 5: Determine how the conflicts should be resolved

- Revise conflict resolution procedures, considering the corporate culture and the nature of the conflict.
- Write a conflict management policy.
- Organize the procedures in the conflict management system.
- Incorporate incentives throughout the conflict management plan.
- Incorporate when and how a positive disciplinary system will be incorporated.

Stage 6: Organize the procedures into a conflict management system

- Develop an Implementation Plan with its own objectives and evaluation mechanisms.

Stage 7: Do the necessary sensitization to ensure that the system is properly executed

Stage 8: Ensure evaluation and adjustment when necessary

Issues specific to undermining, bullying and violence

An advanced issue is the management of undermining, bullying and physical violence, the abatement of which uses the stages above, but which usually require other strategies. As previously stated, organizational leaders should assess their operations to ascertain their people's vulnerability to undermining, bullying and physical violence.

Immunizing the Organization from Undermining

I have already established that undermining is possibly the most difficult and pervasive type of conflict to address. If influential managers sense that undermining is too frequent an occurrence, they may suggest the following:

Ensure as much as realistically possible that rewards are earned and not awarded in return for personal favors. Now this *is* hard, but comprehensive performance assessment systems like 360 degrees help in this regard.

Accept and reject recommendations based upon their merits and demerits rather than on the likeability of the persons who gave them.

Ensure open communication about promotions, new plans, changes, and bad news – this makes it hard for the negative rumors associated with undermining to thrive.

Help others to explain their decisions to help immunize the culture against favoritism and non-favoritism (see also Chapter 9).

Ensure that as many employees as possible learn critical thinking. People tend to undermine best when persons are either too gullible, too cynical and do not assess ideas and information critically (see also Chapter 6).

Some organizational tacticians argue that everyone should be acquainted with political strategies so that everyone is aware when they are being used against them or others. Indeed, I believe that astute employees are increasingly purchasing books like Casey Hawley's *100+ Tactics for Office Politics*,[58] in which she has a section on dirty tricks and ways to counter them. For example:

Dirty Trick: withhold information. One way to make sure you show up unprepared is for the trickster to delay giving you materials and information until the last minute. The trickster can tell your boss that she will pass on the info and then give to to you minutes before a meeting. You will have little time to prepare.

Here are two of the four points that Hawley suggests to counter this form of trickery:

If you suspect materials are delayed, call the sender immediately. Now the trickster looks slipshod.

Say "The information John (the trickster) gave me this morning looks good. Before committing to such a serious task, I'd like to study it a bit more."

Even though the information is very useful, we can discern how much personal energy is usurped by having to play political games because those are the routes to survival or progress. The other problem is that everyone becomes a detective and "trickery" is "unraveled" even where it does not exist. Clearly, the best way to reduce undermining is to open the communication channels and to commit to a culture of respect.

Bullying

Bullying becomes difficult to do when the recommendations below are applied:

Define what is meant by bullying in precise, clear language. An act of bullying is an annoyance to one person and a serious problem to another. Provide concrete illustrations of unacceptable behavior to support the explanation.

Clearly state the organization's position on workplace bullying and its commitment to violence prevention. This statement should ideally come from the CEO.

State the consequences of making threats and other bullying behaviors.

Strongly encourage the reporting of all bullying incidents. Clearly describe the confidential process by which employees can report incidents, to whom they report incidents and how they are expected to responsibly deal with outcomes that they consider positive[59] and negative.

Outline how training and information will be provided to employees.

Commit to provide support services to targets.

It is also recommended that short lists of prohibited behaviors are provided. Rules should be few and should support positive behaviors rather than prohibiting bullying and harassment behaviors. Stating generalities is the bane of many an anti-bullying program and rules should describe specific behaviors.

How the person who bullies is communicated with is very important so that she understands the consequences of her behavior. Saying "you are a bully" may achieve no more than to put the perpetrator on the defensive. It is better to say "your colleagues do not feel safe with you because of your shouting; is their safety important to you?" If a confused or obstinate perpetrator replies that bullying is not a safety issue, then counseling or other measures are in order. If the person responds that the safety of her colleagues *is* important, the following question could be: "how can you encourage them to truly respect you and also ensure their own safety when around you?" Training, as recommended in Chapter 4, may help, and so may discipline, discussed in the following chapter. Nonetheless, some of these perpetrator-types with chronic dysfunctional personalities should be asked to leave the organization, despite whatever talents they may have, because of the tremendous damage that one person can do to the psyches and physical health of others.

Violence

Leaders among the managerial, supervisory and non-supervisory ranks should be trained to recognize conditions that contribute to violence and to properly manage violent situations. Wise organizations actively promote anti-violence in their communities; not only does this stance help the communities, it helps to assure the security of the organization and its people. Every large organization should engage a high profile leader who directly undertakes anti-violence functions.

Anti-Violence and Anti-Bullying Policies

Good anti-violence and anti-bullying programs are supported by specific policies. I recommend one major Anti-Violence Policy with three sub-sections for companies that wish to have an anti-weapons policy, an anti-sexual harassment policy, and an anti-bullying policy. The anti-weapons policy would stipulate who is permitted to be armed and under what circumstances. Definitions of a weapon would be given, including the fact that virtually any hard or sharp object can be utilized as a weapon. Some anti-weapons policies define our limbs as possible weapons – a kick clearly is an act of violence. The anti-sexual harassment and general bullying policies should stipulate whether the human resource manager or a specially appointed person or panel would address those complaints.

I have witnessed significant damage to careers, health and property that well written and properly explained policies, procedures and consequences to behaviors would have helped to avert. Policies and procedures are usually more specific and enforced more stringently than codes of conduct. Managers often ask why there should be policies if people do not always follow them, but the same argument could be applied to national laws. If we had no laws, there would be anarchy. An anti-violence policy, like a code of conduct, will "not prevent the deliberately venal person from violating the law, but will help those who are subject to moral persuasion to obey the law."[60] The term "anti-violence policy" helps employees to understand that repeated bullying, and punishing an individual for not consenting to a sexual act, constitute violence, and that breaches of the code are simply not worth the consequences.

The introduction to the anti-violence policy should note the high costs of violence to the organization and also state applicable regulatory requirements, where possible. The policy needs to make crystal clear the specific procedures for investigating and resolving complaints. The document should also state that a co-ordinating individual or committee exists for conflict resolution, and explain how and why to make a complaint. Notably, policy writers should also be aware that in a particularly unhealthy company, frivolous or mischievous complaints may be made. Therefore the policy should explain both the seriousness of making a complaint, and the seriousness with which frivolous and mischievous complaints will be addressed.[61]

Employees should be advised on policy monitoring and review, and their questions should be patiently responded to. Here are some questions I have heard: If I just raise my voice repeatedly am I to be accused of bullying? If I genuinely believe an employee does not meet the requirements for a promotion, am I being vindictive? What if I have one of those oversensitive employees who feels bullied over everything? I only winked at that man – could his problem be that I reprimanded him last month why I have automatically become a sexual harasser?

Sexual harassment is certainly not always violent. It is contextual. In some societies, pressuring a member of another sex is not perceived as harassment, but as a necessary and approved aspect of persuasion. What constitutes sexual harassment not only needs to be written: examples and role plays would be required for individuals to have a fuller understanding of the policy.

Top Management's Influence

This chapter has showed how values nourish or liquidize the conflict management system. Values assist employees to identify with and commit to organizational goals.

If leaders encourage or deny the existence of an aggressive, intimidating environment, then positive values are eroded. Top management therefore is a most critical component of the organization's ethical climate because they create, reinforce, or modify values according to their own actions. Top management has the onus of forging and practicing values, but quite frankly, other things may be on their minds. Leaders anywhere in the organization can initiate the process towards creating and nourishing values that assure both goal achievement and health, especially if they have the political skill to influence top management. Several strategies have been suggested in this chapter, but the most workable strategies are often those suggested by the organization's people. Fortunately, a reworking of values will be successful, if continuously reinforced by strong leaders.

CHAPTER 4

The Value of Ongoing Learning

The Ritz Carlton and other successful organizations have maintained excellence by providing ongoing learning opportunities to their people. Many reports testify to the significant benefits of effective employee development. For example, in a study of 3,000 companies, researchers found that an investment of 10% of revenue on capital improvements yielded a 3.9% increase in productivity, but a similar investment in developing people increased productivity by 8.5%.[62] Another study reported return on investment results for ten private and public organizations which ranged from 150% to 2000% and averaged 871%, a figure which represented an average of nearly nine dollars gain per dollar invested in learning in those organizations.[63]

Any program that helps an employee to do her work properly assists in abating conflict – for example, we know that just one incompetent or discourteous customer service representative can create a breeding ground for disharmony. If the representative does not possess the requisite technical or attitudinal skills, she must play political games to survive. It is debatable whether blame can be ascribed to her. Fournies discusses fourteen reasons why individuals do not do their jobs at the expected standards. Among the reasons are: individuals do not know *why* they should do the particular job, *how* to do the job or think they are *already* doing it.[64]

Clearly, interpersonal relations are a key factor. Dan Hill states that not understanding how to manage emotions or to accept feedback accounts for 49% of the reasons why new employees fail and that a survey found that only 40% of employees were able to work well with others.[65] This has implications for interpersonal relationships.

But not only formal programs on interpersonal relationships are necessary. About 70% of what an employee needs to know to do his work is learned outside of formal training programs,[66] and employees learn from each other more than any other method. Ichijo speaks of about "tacit knowledge" which is essentially "how things are done around here."[67] For this reason, if the organization has serious conflict issues, meetings should be held on a monthly or quarterly basis to sort out the conflicts that get in the way of productivity and good service. It is useful to have an experienced employee conduct part of meetings dealing with conflict – that individual is likely to influence colleagues because of the respect that he or she enjoys in the organization.

Where violence is concerned, many employees are quite knowledgeable in specific safety or violence prevention issues and are willing to share this information with colleagues. If trained how to train, security experts such as the police or military are excellent resources: they cite their actual experiences in perceptivity, restraint, and errors of judgment. They save lives and are enormous assets to organizations.

Reorientations for Leaders

It is impossible to separate conflict management from leadership. Regular effective leadership and management courses, seminars, mentorship programs and communities of learning should be regular and ongoing, to develop the prowess required to prevent and resolve organizational and individual performance problems. Companies with limited funding can still arrange for leaders to purchase high quality articles or books, and hold monthly or bi-monthly discussions on these readings.

Leaders do wonders by learning how to transfer successful interpersonal relations practices to others, paving the way for the collective learning that will eventually drive the change. Training-oriented organizations sensitize their leaders upon employment to successful leadership practices and principles. Retreats, meetings and seminars are useful ways to conduct orientations and re-orientations.

Reorientations suggest learning a new way of acting and being for employees. Though I use the term "reorientation" to show what the activity actually is, I recognize that the term has militaristic or propagandist tones, and an organization may want to use a more palatable term congruent with its values or mission statement. The reorientation needs to be grounded in a philosophy, a word or a term. If the word "excellence" has been liberally used previously but with minimal effect, another term should be chosen, because "excellence" is now associated with "mediocrity". The reorientation also needs to be grounded in a no-blame format, largely because blame incurs stress and stress impairs learning. Even stress lasting a few hours can impair brain-cell communication in the brain's learning and memory region.[68]

Good reorientations provide opportunities for questions to be raised. For example, facilitators will find that some participants do not fully understand the impact of bullying. Leaders have asked: "why are we so concerned when we have a large number of employees and only a few bullies in the workplace?" If the leaders are asked "are the bullies successful?" they reply either "mostly yes" or "sometimes". If asked "what is the cost to the company?" they reply "high". I explain to them that having three (mostly) successful bullies in the workplace suggests that the other 297 do not know how to address the costly problem.

Here's the formula.

$ Not understanding how destructive conflicts affect market share, return on assets and stock return + continued actions that reflect this misunderstanding > $ Time spent in the learning that leads to action.

Once managers understand the formula, they are generally eager to provide examples that speak to the accuracy of the formula.

The stages used for effective training would be employed for reorientations, that is, identifying the specific training needs in tandem with the organization's objectives, designing the training, delivering the training, and evaluating the training at various levels.[69] Optimally, learning programs are held in an environment that allows participants to reflect and plan to create something excellent, before returning to the organization to execute the plans. The orientation should be conducted in groups of no more than 12 participants, to permit the participants to feel more comfortable questioning assumptions, thereby developing a richer understanding of the topic at hand. Here are two illustrations of reorientation exercises.

Reorientation Exercise 1: Reflective Questions that align conflict management with the marketing function

This exercise aligns the marketing function with good conflict management.[70] The basic understanding of the marketing function is this: if we don't sell a good product or provide a good service, we're in trouble. The exercise reinforces the value of marketing in addition to developing a comprehension of the way in which conflict confounds the marketing function.

Here is a sample of reflective questions that could be asked of managers:

* *How do you treat everyone in this company if everyone has an important marketing role?*

- *What would the best organizations do?*

- *What would the best organizations not do?*

  If we don't know the answers to any of these questions, what should we do?

- *Do all employees understand how valued they are as brand managers? If not, what do we do?*

- *What would the best organizations do?*

- *What would the best organizations not do?*

- *If we don't know the answers to any of these questions, what should we do?*

- *How do we all support each other to ensure that everyone knows they have an important marketing role?*

- *If we do not have a lot of money, what is the best we can do?*

Managers are asked to complete their answers to the questions before the orientation meeting starts, since reflection is required before the discussion starts. An orchestra of sighs may be heard when they first look at the questions but they will become animated when discussing the responses. You will get responses such as this one: "They never taught us marketing like this in business school!"

Reflective Questions can be used for any area, for example:

Managing Conflict (General): How do you manage conflict? How do your methods/strategies help to resolve the conflict? What in your opinion are the worst ways to manage challenging interpersonal situations? How do you discuss a dispute with a colleague before it reaches a more advanced stage? Where would you go to get help? How do you document a conflict appropriately?

Active Discrimination: Which groups do you feel most empathetic to and why? Do you feel the same towards all groups? How does discrimination affect your work and the work of your supervisees? Are there any challenges to the organization's emphasis on diversity? How should we deal with those challenges? What are the opportunities of working in a diverse culture?

Physical Violence: Have you ever had an incident of physical violence in your department? Did anyone see the signs? What should be done when employees seem to be particularly angry or "tight"? How does the anti-violence policy state you should act in these circumstances? What does the anti-violence policy say about how victims should be treated? How should secondary victims, (those who witnessed the violence), be treated?[71]

After each reflective exercise, it is recommended that participants be involved in exercises that help them to establish commonalities of purpose and to respect differences, thereby assisting them to be more appreciative of each other. And because reflective exercises utilize high levels of mental energy, stress-busting breaks or fun exercises should be introduced during the meeting. Fun and breaks also help the participants to bond. In many national cultures, it is also important that decent food is provided – though not too much so that they become phlegmatic after lunch. This is not a minor point – good food will energize not only their bodies but their spirits!

Reorientation Exercise 2 - Analysis of Statements

Facilitators choose statements that they feel will elicit vibrant and thoughtful discussion among their fellow participants, and also ask participants to initiate discussion topics that are relevant to their work culture. Facilitators will find that the majority of managers enjoy this kind of exercise. Examples of reflective questions are given below:

General question – *If we think of ourselves as strong, wise and capable, how do we act? We need examples!*

Question and activity for physical violence – "the prophet" – You know that someone will enter the organization to injure an employee next month, and you have the means to prevent it. What would you do now? Provide as much detail as possible.

Questions and activities for bullying prevention. This exercise is not about transporting ourselves to fictional territories like the last question, but is an actual statement made by a manager who was armed with an MBA. The manager who made the statement below had attended several courses, but in her own words, the courses only taught her what to do, not what *not* to do. This is the statement that she made which has both elements of fear and bullying:

The Statement: *I know everything that is being said about me in this organization: I have my sources everywhere – if anybody says anything bad about me, they're in trouble!*

Managers should look at the advantages and disadvantages of the statement and finish completing the table below.

Possible Advantages to Manager *Examples*	Possible Disadvantages to Manager *Examples*	Possible Advantages to Providers of Information *Examples*	Possible Disadvantages to Providers of Information *Examples*
Manager lets employees know that she is powerful enough to have sources everywhere (even if the statement is a bluff, it could still leave that impression).	The person bringing the news could manipulate the manager to further her own interests by telling not only truths, but half truths, falsehoods, or taking the information out of context.	A benefit in return for the information.

Other employees recognizing that the he/she is a favorite. | Unless doing something to get fellow employees in trouble is completely in line with his nature, the source would secretly dislike the manager, and would need to be careful to continue the pretense of loyalty. |
| Letting everyone know it is not wise to say anything bad about her without it being taken to a source. | The manager may make poor decisions if they are based on false or half true information. | | There are political consequences in being seen as the news carrier if not completely protected by the manager. |
| May be a route to further power, if power in that organization increases with employee fear. | Possibility of giving information to a "double-spy" – such persons thrive in undermining cultures. | | |

Questions for Undermining

If you assess the statement made by this lady, you will probably conclude that it is an immature one. Much conflict (though of course not all) is in fact adolescent behavior – *and herein lies the major problem.* One lady told me after being admonished by a manager in his twenties "I am a grandmother, therefore I am grown up, he should not have spoken to me that way." The unhappy fact was that the young man was viewed by others in the organization to be more emotionally mature than she was. He was admired for addressing her undermining manouevers which were girl-like in nature. But what is really being grown-up? Perhaps employees should really have a great debate on how to elevate the organization into true adulthood!

Negative gossip, a key undermining strategy, can be done fairly innocently. The purpose of the exercise is not the elimination of all gossip (impossible, anyway), and certainly, not all gossip is egregious but basically, a sharing of information. Actually, a University of Liverpool evolutionary psychologist has found that academics at a university dining room spent *70 percent of the time talking about one another:* topics which should contain ideas, politics, religion, ethics, culture and work rated only 2 or 3 percent. Studies suggest that gossip in the workplace is negative only 5% of the time, most people understanding that when a person spreads malicious gossip, the listeners unconsciously attribute similar negative traits to the speaker.[72]

The manager may opt to read a section of a book with her team on negative gossip or on any other potential conflict-producing behavior. For example, here is a thought-eliciting passage from Richard Carlson's *Don't Sweat the Small Stuff at Work*:[73]

> The next time you hear someone backstabbing someone else, try to imagine how the offending person actually feels beneath the confident, secure appearance. How does it feel to say nasty, offensive, and negative things about someone else who isn't even there to defend themselves? Obviously, that's a loaded question – but the answer is so obvious that it's almost embarrassing to discuss. I know that when I have backstabbed in the past, my words have left me with an uncomfortable feeling. I remember asking myself the question how could you stoop so low? You simply can't win. You may get a moment or two of relief from getting something off your chest, but you have to live with your words for the rest of the day – and longer.

Preaching about negative gossip rarely works – gossip can be delicious and take us momentarily out of the doldrums of the average work day. Here are some reflective questions about partaking in negative gossip. The reader may be surprised at their simplicity – nonetheless, a lot of us have given little thought to the reasons, mechanics and results of negative gossip:

- Did the speaker who shared the gossip feel the gossip would be appreciated? If yes, why?

- Did the listeners appreciate the speaker in any way for giving them this information in this way?[74] If yes, why?

- Is it human to feel *schadenfreude*[75] when a colleague is down, and if so, does it make one feel more successful?

- Would the listeners gossip about the sharer of the gossip in a similar manner if she were in any form of distress?

- Would the speaker also say the same things about the listeners if they were in distress?

- How factual do you think the gossip is based on the person who told it?

- Why can gossip lead to problems if it is spread?

- What are other ways to share information that allow for the dignity of all employees?

It is helpful to blend exercises like these with cases of how managers have been able to help their teams.

Conflict Management Courses and Related Information

A course outlining the general principles of conflict management and prevention will benefit the management and supervisory population. The training provides the participants with a solid grounding on basic conflict resolution strategies and the various forms and genres of conflict – which, as previously stated, is not limited to undermining, bullying and physical violence. The conflict management jargon is growing, and every year sees a growth in terminology. Rather than conflate participations with the vernacular in vogue, it is more important to provide participants with adequate time to practice, as it is the *supervised practice* that is critical in conflict management training.

Subjects that allow us to understand and control the tougher forms of conflict include the prevention and management of highly political behavior, bullying and physical violence – and the extreme, which is psychopathic behavior. Psychopaths are particularly charming, seemingly normal, and wreak havoc, and arguably constitute about 5-10% percent of the population anywhere – in some populations perhaps higher. Because they appear so normal, not everyone can discern their strategies. The following is a statement made by Martha Stout in Jon Ronson's book "The Psychopath Test".

> "As a group they tend to be more charming than most people," she said. "They have no warm emotions of their own but will study the rest of us. They're the boss or coworker who likes to make other people jump just for the pleasure of seeing them jump. They're the spouse who marries to look socially normal but inside the marriage shows no love after the initial charm wears off."[76]

This "charm" element of psychopaths (also known as sociopaths) I have also noticed. I have had close encounters with two persons whom I consider to be psychopathic, one in a professional capacity. Both were charismatic. This is not to say, of course, that all charming people are psychopathic or that all persons who are not charming are not.

In Martha Stout's own book *The Sociopath Next Door*, she discusses our inability or unwillingness to see these dangerous traits. She asks and responds to a profound question:

"Why are conscience-bound human beings so blind? And why are they so hesitant to defend themselves, and the ideals and people they care about, from the minority of people who possess no conscience at all? A large part of the answer has to do with the emotions and thought processes that occur in us when we are confronted with sociopathy. We are afraid, and our sense of reality suffers. We think we are imagining things, or exaggerating, or that we ourselves are somehow responsible for the sociopath's behavior."[77]

It is beneficial if even a few managers and supervisors in large organizations are trained to discern the signs of psychopathic behavior. Other useful information is the management of anger, disappointment and envy. There is an understandable reluctance for managers responsible for training to address possibly disturbing themes such as these within the context of an existing training program, and it would need to be done carefully so as not to overwhelm the participants with too much material that appears to be cast in the shadows. In other words, the participants should receive what I call "sun and light" courses but some information on human failings (even our own) could protect us from great harm, which is the very reason why we tell children not to go with strangers.

Let's look at envy. There are too few courses and seminars addressing an emotion that is so often obsessive. The quote below is apt:

"Envy may be the subtlest – perhaps I should say the most insidious — of the seven deadly sins. Surely it is the one that people are least likely to want to own up to, for to do so is to admit that one is probably ungenerous, mean, small-hearted. It may also be the most endemic. Apart from Socrates, Jesus, Marcus Aurelius, Saint Francis, Mother Teresa, and only a few others, at one time or another, we have all felt flashes of envy, even if in varying intensities, from its minor pricks to its deep, soul-destroying, lacerating stabs." [78]

This statement is from Joseph Epstein's refreshingly honest book on envy. Epstein chronicles his own experience of envy, which, fortunately for him and his colleagues, did not progress to the malicious forms of envy. He states "professional achievement, I noticed, seemed to bring out intramural envy. For many years the three best art critics in America didn't speak to one another."

I believe that we should learn about envy, not to berate ourselves even if we are very envious, and learn how to better manage this form of anger. Envy spurs us to achieve goals or damage ourselves and others – or all of these. We may wish some people very well – for example, athletes whose victories bring honor to the community. However, we may also be disposed to find faults in the houses of our neighbors that would be barely noticeable if we did not envy them.

Those of us who derive great enjoyment from being envied often envy at a similar level. Unfortunately, it is also common in the workplace to think that other persons do not like us because they envy us when our actions encourage others to distance themselves from us, physically or emotionally.

People who are otherwise reasonable and generous can suffer from envy, particularly when they think the envied persons do not deserve their happiness, possessions or status. The envier suffers from more intense feelings when he or she has worked equally hard as the envied person, but with less buoyant results.

Interestingly, research has found that persons are more likely to lie to a person they envy in the workplace than to a person they do not envy, so there is clearly some correlation between deception and envy. This research has critical implications for the workplace, as deception induces stress. Deception threatens the deceiver's perception as a trustworthy person and stimulates emotions such as guilt.[79]

I was informed of a situation where several female workers were being laid off at an organization, including 'Susan', who felt she was targeted because she had not slept with the manager. "Felt" being the operative word because she had no evidence to back her assertions. Susan said of her former coworker 'Joan' who had remained on the job, "well, at least I kept my body, and bad things will happen to her." When Susan later realized that Joan was still working and thriving, she issued other statements that suggested potent envy.

Susan's "Joan syndrome" might be reactivated among female coworkers in a future job. They might wonder why she is so onerous – but she is unable to manage her envy and disappointment that now appears to be embedded in her psyche. Imagine how much happier she and her coworkers would be if she were able to control her envy! Thankfully, organizations with healthy cultures tend to mitigate festering emotional wounds like obsessive envy.

Employees are so vibrantly engaged in their work that they have other things on their minds.

Even if a seminar is called *Bringing Joy into the Company*, it should incorporate a few of the harder subjects. I believe that pure "sun and light" have a transient impact. We also need to understand and perhaps manage the most challenging employees – and even the "dark sides" in ourselves, which tend to become more apparent in hard, unyielding times.

In courses that address human failings in some part, it is recommended that class size be relatively small since ample time is required for role play. For example, where violent persons are concerned, participants should role play coming from a position of strength that does not involve shouting or abuse. Participants would also learn how one's posture and demeanor help or mar violence prevention. Consider this statement by Duran and Nasci:

> "Compliance is usually best gained by being forceful and authoritative, without being insulting or derogatory. Everything you say can affect your situation. Your voice is a tool that you have at your disposal and should be thought of that way. By using it properly you can diffuse situations, calm people down, and you may even be able to resolve potentially violent situations peacefully. On the other hand, if you do not choose your words carefully, you may escalate a situation..."[80]

Alternatively, though we know that anyone can be attacked, employees should take care not to adopt a "victim stance". Grossman and Christensen state that: "the vast majority said that they specifically targeted victims by body language: slumped walk, passive behavior and lack of awareness. They chose their victims like big cats do in Africa, when they select one out of the herd that is least able to protect itself."[81]

There are other seminars and courses that can have great impact on organizational morale and productivity, especially when based on positive psychology principles. Most training to reduce hard conflict also makes use of cognitive behavioral modification (CBM), which refers to a wide array of techniques to modify behaviour and covert thoughts by teaching employees how to actively participate in identifying and understanding their own thoughts. If done correctly and with cultural sensitivity, CBM helps to oxygenate the working environment.

Finally, learning organizations ensure that course and seminar attendees write a plan on how to transfer the competencies acquired from learning interventions to their jobs.

CHAPTER 5

Somebody to Talk to

Fortunately, employees' work lives have been positively turned around by managers who listen to their difficulties. However, not every employee wants to discuss financial problems with their managers (as they would to a financial coach), or how serious family issues affect their mood at work (as they might to a therapist) or if a strongly-allied colleague is bullying them (as they would to an ombudsman). Having a helping professional to talk to is therefore an important part of a strong integrated conflict management system.

Little of this is cheap of course. Few organizations employ therapists but organizations may have a group health insurance policy that provides for the services of therapists. Management in smaller organizations should advise staff about able therapists who charge moderate fees, and explain that the stigma of visiting a therapist is either passé or should well be. Coaches are not usually as expensive as therapists, and can be of benefit to emotionally healthy employees. Fortunately, most medium sized organizations can afford to train at least one manager as a coach. Though not every company can afford an ombudsman, some companies train key employees to become mediators. Fortunately, in most countries, small and medium sized businesses have access to organizations which offer professional mediation services.

Ombudsmen - independent mediators

By using the term ombudsman, I am also referring to persons who may not have the job title but who assume that role as all or part of their job function. Good ombudsmen act as independent referees between the organization's people, and are indispensible in large organizations. The offices of ombudsmen (referred to as ombuds in the singular and plural) should physically reside outside of the organization to afford them a psychological distance from conflicts: if ombuds are internal, they are expected to reside outside the four cultural walls, hard but not impossible to do.

The best formal or informal ombuds are perceived to enjoy a high level of integrity. Non-attorney ombuds usually have access to legal counsel. An ombuds also needs access to a team of trained neutrals, since it is difficult for a single ombuds to play all of the roles required for complex mediations. For example, for mediation among teams, the ombuds can focus on policy issues, while another mediator helps the participants to build positive relationships.

Excellent ombuds save organizations time and a huge amount of money. For example, it is common practice for ombuds to encourage clients not to abuse their productive energy by ruminating on a problem, but to reappraise conflicts in various ways, such as trying to see the situation from the other party's perspective. Excellent ombuds also find strategies to resolve conflicts even when neither party particularly wants the conflict to be resolved.

Ombuds sometimes make controversial decisions, as seen in this case where a worker, 'Louis', had threatened a human resource manager, a departmental manager and two supervisors in a company located near a community plagued by violence. Louis had said "If I'm fired, I know where you and your children live." The person acting in the role of ombuds, 'Joseph', arranged for Louis to be placed on contract, and a couple of months after that, arranged for that contract to be dissolved due to executive decision. This ensured that it was the faceless "top management" that was responsible for Louis exiting the company and not the managers and supervisors that he could identify. Joseph's decision was not considered correct by everyone – some felt that he should have called the police immediately regardless of the threats issued, but he stood by his decision. After Louis left the company, Joseph helped management to initiate anti-violence procedures.

The Need for Therapy

My observation of the average large and medium-sized workplace suggests that at least 5% of the population requires therapy for anger-related issues. Yet individuals may work hard whilst suffering from anger or depression (anger turned inward). Some individuals undergoing depression are called lazy, but they are not. Depression is a physical illness. The hippocampus of the depressed is often smaller than persons who do not suffer from depression, referred to as hippocampal atrophy.

Employees requiring therapy the most may attend sessions for any variety of reasons, and the benefits of therapy need to be sold to them. It's not only about their conflicts at work, but difficulties at home. It is a myth that we divorce work from home. Unhappy employees attempt to lock up top-of-mind feelings such as worry about an alcoholic spouse at home or a child taking illegal drugs. Emotions seemingly under lock and key break out to affect the texture of virtually every action and behavior.

Individuals use repression or silence as their only conscious or unconscious strategy because they are just not coping or don't have anyone to talk to.[82] Repression has the potential to injure the peace in the organization and incur costs. Repression impacts health. A study looked at the illnesses associated with repression, using a survey of approximately 24,000 respondents. The 22% of females and 11% of males who reported having a traumatic sexual experience before age 17 (but who had not previously discussed this with anyone), were more likely to have a variety of health problems, including but not limited to, high blood pressure, ulcers and the flu.[83]

Since the mind affects the body, therapists could be considered to be both mental and physical health professionals. They help the client to relax to the extent where conversation flows easily, and assist the client to arm herself with the psychological competencies to resolve a problem or to co-exist with a problem until it is resolved.

Therapists also assist the client to develop a set of realistic and satisfying goals.

Different individuals require different kinds of therapists and therapy. A verbally abusive employee may need a specialist in anger management.[84] Many therapists ask the client to respond to a set of questions individually crafted for him, and focus on the emotions that box out every new refreshing plan that the client may think of. A focus on negative emotions may be necessary to genuinely overcome or manage trauma and grow as a mentally healthy human being. According to Niederhoffer and Pennebaker "one cannot ascribe too much importance to positivity by neglecting what appears to be a necessary psychological cost."[85]

An expert therapist has the experience to intuitively know what repeated or singular memories to elicit and how to assist in their integration. Or perhaps not dredge up a particularly painful memory, depending on the individual and circumstance. There are several protocols and methods that address painful methods but also help the client to become a well integrated, functional individual. [86]

Therapists may even need to gently nudge clients out of the newest fads of thinking. Not feeling guilt has become popular in much of the popular literature because of guilt's role in robbing us of happiness. Though guilt can be an unnecessary burden, various forms of atonement are recommended once deliberate and significant harm has been done to another individual. I once referred a client in her fifties to a therapist when she spoke about experiencing deep pain from her childhood in addition to claiming she could bully without remorse "because everybody knows guilt is bad."

Anyone who *enjoys* seriously harming others – whether through undermining, bullying or physical violence – is a prime candidate for therapy. Medication helps clients with a strong predilection to physical violence, which means that psychiatric care is required. Of note, a study has shown that persons with severe mental illness exhibited higher rates of violence comparative to other community members. Mental illness defined in this study included major depression, panic, mania, obsessive-compulsive and bipolar disorder, schizophrenia, alcohol and drug abuse or dependence, and phobia.[87] Notably, employees can enter the workplace as reasonably integrated but become substance abusers, for example, for any number of reasons.

Organizations summarily dismiss employees who initiate a physically violent episode at work, but the victims and secondary victims can be helped considerably by therapy. Few organizations can afford individual therapists for all secondary victims, but following a deliberate action that results in death or critical injury, a therapist should be engaged to respond to the questions of employees.

Coaching

Coaches, unlike therapists, do not use psychological approaches to heal deep-rooted emotional scars. Coaches lend their support by using expert listening and questioning techniques to help emotionally healthy clients to navigate between the shoals of challenging decisions.

In addition, coaches provide creative templates for effective future action. I believe that coaching helps clients who perform the milder forms of bullying and undermining because it helps them to discover more potent and intelligent ways by which to achieve their goals.

Coaching works. The Blanchard report states that 92% of persons coached in organizations felt highly satisfied with the coaching experience and that 86% felt that both they and the organization were reaping significant benefits from the coaching.[88] Coaches bring to the fore positive but realistic ideas that the individual had not previously thought of. Coaches help the client to commit to reaching a goal by discovering untapped resources in themselves. Most coaches take the stress out of "achieving the goal" (which can be so stressful that some clients won't even bother to try in the first place). Instead, coaches encourage the client to enjoy the exciting ride towards goal achievement.

The creative client might wish to express himself on paper using a form of Chiaroscuro, an Italian term used in art for the contrast between light and darkness. Visually–oriented individuals are asked what they can do to increase the quality of daylight in their departments. Creative audio-oriented persons are asked to hear the amount of light or darkness they want in the departmental band or orchestra. It is remarkable what some people will say after visualizing or hearing the problem as light and darkness, than when only words are used.

Positive Psychology and Other Trends

Much therapy and coaching is done under the aegis of positive psychology, an approach developed by Martin Seligman and Christopher Peterson. Positive psychology looks at what works well rather than analyzing dysfunction, and is based on scientific evidence. Areas of focus include benefit-finding, the integration of one's life and work with one's values and finding happiness. Benefit finding is an important coping strategy. A study showed that persons with daily pain and who had found benefits from their illness at the start of a study reported fewer days on which their activities were affected by their pain than those who found no benefits at all from their pain.[89] Benefit-finding is helpful when an individual is disappointed with the outcome of a conflict. Weaving benefit finding and other positive values into work promotes work effectiveness in addition to the engagement or happiness which is a universal goal.

The majority of clients will thrive under a positive-psychology approach. Other approaches may be used with individuals who are not motivated by goals of happiness, but who basically live in other existential paradigms. Julie Norem makes a case for the hidden benefits to "defensive pessimism", which she refers to as "a defensive strategy that helps us to work through our anxious thoughts rather than denying them, so that we may achieve our goals" (p. 3). High achievers are not always optimists, suggesting that the low levels of achievement ascribed to pessimism do not apply to all the pessimists. Norem also argues that "defensive pessimists" have built very satisfying lives by confronting their shadow sides.[90]

Optimism has shades and textures – from misguided optimism to practical optimism. Misguided optimism leads to disappointment and depression.[91] Stockdale, while a prisoner-of-war, developed a variety of coping strategies, including faith without resorting to the optimism which would have been inappropriate under the circumstances. The optimists who expected to be out of the POW camps by certain times died of a broken heart. Misguided optimism can lead to depression and emotional paralysis. Combining hopefulness with reality generally produced much better results, [92] [93] and is a good strategy for dealing with conflicts where one or both parties are not happy with the resolution.

Helping Professionals looking at the clients' values in tandem with their environments

The manager or educator who reads this book has usually coached in some way, and is therefore a part-time helping professional. Good helping professionals understand cultural realities. People of course live in a broader culture than the one provided at the workplace, and behaviors are judged right or wrong based on their agreement with the culture and the sub-culture to which the person belongs. Our core values of course are not only a consequence of our genetic predispositions but can also alter according to the environment to which we belong – aptly expressed by the forensic psychiatrist Robert Simon:

"Good men and women are far from perfect in their behaviors. We are neither all good nor all bad. To varying degrees, we are a combination of both. An unexpected situation may become the occasion for one side or the other to win out. Combat, for example, may incite acts of heroism or cowardice from the same person, depending on the circumstances. In peace time, a former sadistic concentration camp guard may slip into the role of the respected but feared cop on the beat.

The basic difference between what is socially considered to be bad and good people is not one of kind, but one of degree, and of the ability of the bad to translate dark impulses into dark actions…Anyone can become violent, even murderous under certain circumstances. Therapists who have undergone their own psychoanalysis or insight psychotherapy have a humanistic recognition of the universality of human intrapsychic experience. These therapists acknowledge in themselves many of the same psychological struggles they find in their patients and in others. It is hoped that therapists handle their personal problems better more of the time, but this is not necessarily so. Dr. Thomas G. Gutheil, Professor of Psychiatry at Harvard and a famed forensic psychiatrist, candidly acknowledges what most therapists know about themselves: "But for the grace of my defenses, there go I."[94]

We adapt to our cultures and there is a debate whether ethical relativism is increasing in most societies. It is our decision whether to march on the road in tune with society's proudest mores, to slide surreptitiously on the road not in tune with society's mores, or to travel on either as convenient. Some clients, especially those with traditional values, want to discuss ethical dilemmas with helping professionals: they find it difficult to raise such subjects even with the dearest family members or friends who, as one executive put it, "look at you as though something is wrong with you."

A manager advised me that he deliberately chose to "give most of his better values a holiday" in order to rapidly get ahead in the particular environment in which he lived. It is arguable whether we need to be ruthless to get to the top. This ruthlessness may be later valued by the society if the person in question eventually changes many lives for the better – which he did. He was a star. Today there are more "stars" in all the various professions and careers than ever before, and more ambition as well. As someone said to me who listens to a program which features prominent individuals "hell, *I* can do that – I can exaggerate what I went through too – and if I got their breaks, I'd have done better!"

I believe that most individuals prefer to take the route of integrity to achieve their goals, even if they occasionally falter. Other individuals are convinced that their high level of aggression toward people who can do little or nothing to help them achieve their goals, has somehow assisted them to get ahead more quickly than if they had progressed through the more conventional routes. Those who succeed with this version of working smart may have heard the truism "the same quality that got you ahead can be the same quality that brings you down." But it is not always a given to know when to stop doing something at which we have been successful for so long.

Beneficial and harmful actions are often juxtaposed in interesting fashions. A person who practised negative organizational politics defended his actions with the statement "I help disabled people" and mentioned his helping organization. Clients may also say "I'm a good father so I'm a good person" or "compared to what I do or who I am after work, this is mild". All of us will sometimes justify an action that was unkind or just foolish.[95] This is important so that we do not torment ourselves with wrong decisions we may have made. Persons who have unnecessarily harmed others may say "I don't regret anything in my life." According to Tarvis and Aronson:

> "As fallible human beings, all of us share the impulse to justify ourselves and avoid taking responsibility for any action that turn out to be harmful, immoral or stupid. …whether the consequences of our mistakes are trivial or tragic, on a small or a national canvas, most of us find it difficult, if not impossible, to say "I was wrong, I made a terrible mistake." The higher the stakes – emotional, financial, moral – the greater the difficulty."

The authors say that when people are provided with evidence showing that they were in error, they do not change their minds, but are more determined than ever to justify the action.[96] The more costly a decision, the more the person is likely to defend it in order to reduce cognitive dissonance, and it is highly likely that cognitive dissonance is more of a feature in highly political organizations than in other organizations. Our own personal values can also clash, giving rise to an armory of complicated behaviors, beyond our own understanding.

What we do know for certain is that people do not want to be mistreated. They generally want to appear strong and in charge of their lives, and will not necessarily admit to being a target or bully, though they will admit to being cautious or assertive. This terminology is perfectly understandable – describing ourselves in euphemistic ways serves to protect our psyches. We do not particularly want others to see our lives associated with a nasty work conflict.

Only by trusting a helping professional will the battered, confused and remorseful come forward. Giving expression to the toxicity clogging their minds will be a great relief in and of itself. The helping professional assists clients to gradually edge out of the cognitive dissonance that keeps them in unconstructive tension or stalemate at work, and to find those values that make them feel most complete as human beings. Helping professionals also help the clients to identify or revaluate their values and assist the clients to navigate between *competing* values – an area which has not been sufficiently addressed.

The organizational culture supports the helping professional by promoting the kind of interpersonal relationships that result in a multiplier effect of benevolence. As previously discussed, the organization molds a certain culture to bring out the best possible in everyone – becoming oases or partial oasis – from what may be stark realities in the outside world.

Martin Seligman shares his powerful perspective on positive psychology:

"Positive psychology makes people happier. Teaching positive psychology, researching positive psychology, using positive psychology in practice as a coach or therapist, giving positive psychology exercises to tenth graders in a classroom, teaching a classroom, parenting little kids with positive psychology. Teaching drill sargeants how to teach about post-traumatic growth, meeting with other positive psychologists, and just reading about positive psychology all make people happier. The people who work in positive psychology are the people with the highest well-being I have ever known."[97]

Expert Listening

Employees certainly do not always need to talk to a therapist or coach. A trained and *perceptive* manager-mediator is a powerful force.

There are joys in this business. A trained listener steps in, does the necessary work, and it's almost hey-presto, that's resolved. There are, of course, the more difficult cases where the individual or group prefers the conflict to remain unresolved – a conflict or a batch thereof can become an individual's *raison d étre*, and a particularly smart individual can play with an untrained mediator like a cat with a mouse.

Two cases are described below: the first case was only moderately challenging - the second was a lot tougher. I also include some general experiences I have had with persons who threaten physical violence.

Case 1 – Bob did not bully anyone

A manager, 'Bob', did not bully anyone. He was distant but respectful. Bob ignored the evidence that one of his workers was verbally assaulting another on a regular basis. He blamed the target, thereby applying double-punishment to the target and awarding himself with a rationalization for doing nothing about the problems in his department. He did not realize that blaming an innocent target is another form of bullying, and said:

> "Why must we mother-coddle big people so much these days? We expect everyone to love us, not realizing that the workplace is just that – the workplace –and I wish people would find friendship and love somewhere else instead of expecting the workplace to be a big fat nursery. Once upon a time you came to work, you did a good job, you put up with a bad boss, you went home."

In Bob's opinion, the conflict should not exist, and he felt bound to ignore it. Through questioning, I encouraged him to explain why protecting an innocent person from bullying is not a matter of friendship or mother-coddling, but developing and maintaining a workplace that promotes dignity. We related it to the treatment of other innocent persons in the society, where others may feel more compassion for the perpetrator – such as a drunken driver – than for the target. That Bob understood clearly. Bob, not blessed with great imagination, found it virtually impossible to put himself in the shoes of what he regarded as incompetent, weak or generally inferior others. It thoroughly annoyed him that so many adults in that workplace acted like children "these days", and he did not believe that he should be supervising children because he had not elected to work in day-care. It took a few discussions with Bob before he understood that the bullying was a problem affecting work in his department and therefore affecting his own performance.

When communicating with an employee, it is best to try and see the conflict from his perspective. It might have been easier for Bob to blame the victim than to admit his fear of getting into a conflict with the perpetrator. Bob who was about 59 or 60 might have said to himself "why should I get into any conflict – I'm a few years to retirement, let me focus on getting my pension and nothing else." He might also fear being the hero. He saw bullying occurring elsewhere and nothing was done. So why does *he* have to be the one to do something about it?[98] When there are many observers, in our case here "observing managers", the personal responsibility of each observer is reduced.[99]

Bob worked in an organizational culture where there were no anti-violence heroes. It is difficult to be the only anti-violence hero in a company that devalues such protagonists. We do not like what we see but are happy that at least it isn't us. We certainly don't want to take on a perpetrator at a higher job classification, a powerful peer, or a very influential employee who reports to us. Most of us like to blend in – and don't like the idea of people who accepted us for being one of them suddenly turning on us for being different! Being the sole proponent of anti-violence in an organization is not usually recommended. There *will* be individuals with excellent political acumen who will start and continue the process almost single handedly, or who have been given permission by the executive team to initiate the process. Even if an individual initiates the process, he should inspire a team to help implement and evaluate the plans. It's much harder to scare a team.

Also, resolving knotty conflicts appeals to few. It's lovely when conflicts just go away and we remember with fondness the very few that actually did disappear all by themselves. Managers who do not have conflict resolution skills do not know how to prevent or to handle episodes of behavior that smacks of adolescent bickering – *You did that, yes you did* and *no, I did not say that, You never liked me from the minute you saw me!* They find themselves impatient with this kind of wrangling, especially if they have that urgent report to produce or want to pursue a creative idea. Since they do not have the required skills, or do not have anyone to help them, they allow the conflict to continue.

A recent survey by the training and organizational performance consulting firm Vitalsmarts found that 93% of workers are negatively affected by inability to deal with conflict on the job; 69% of workers avoid confronting coworkers on issues of accountability, and 50% say they shy away from confrontations for fear of a negative outcome. Some are afraid of making enemies in the workplace, others do not want to get into arguments and others fear they will lose their jobs as a result of trying to deal with conflict. "I'm amazed that at all levels of the company people need conflict management skills and don't have them," said Nancy Helgeson, a career coach and psychologist in San Diego.

"Part of the reason is a lack of confidence," said Joseph Grenny, president of Vitsmarts and author of the book *Crucial Conversations*. "People feel that they don't have the skills to resolve the conflict, so they try to just ignore it." The results can be devastating. Inability to deal with conflicts means that problems go unresolved, workers are unhappy and work performance and productivity are undermined."[100]

Case 2: Undermining of a Supervisor

Many years ago, I was advised by an executive that a promising individual who had managed a store for only six months, was already threatening to leave because of the attitude of four of the sales assistants. The executive informed me that the company would "just love" to get rid of the four ladies, but wouldn't because of the large redundancy packages that would be needed to be paid to them. I was tempted to refuse the assignment, but understood that perfect companies are as rare as perfect humans, and knew that all problems cannot be fully resolved but "improved".

The ladies in question must have known that they were basically superfluous staff, further compounding the problem. They were still in the most junior position of sales assistant after over two decades of working in the company. They had watched their fellow sales assistants being promoted to supervisors or members of office staff over the years, and had observed themselves in woeful stalemate.

I was a very young woman who felt stuck with four dour middle aged women who seemed to enjoy putting the taint of cynicism on every enthusiastic comment I made. In hindsight, I overdid the enthusiastic stuff, more liking the way it *sounded* than really caring about its impact on my weary and wary middle aged listeners.

The good decision that I made was to ask the general manager if I could speak to these older sales assistants without the younger sales assistants present. When we were alone, I asked "what should I have said in the workshop that would have made sense to you?" After this bit of humility on my part, they started to talk, a bit tentatively at first. Then came the spate of complaints. They shared the real or perceived injustices meted out to them over the years, and in essence felt caricaturized by the circumstances of their work life. Yet a liveliness emanated in the room. Relevance had taken centre stage, not just professional behavior to customers, (which was irrelevant to them because they did not like the company). After their anger had been released, two of them actually smiled.

I was particularly interested in one story. 'Jill' said "I was to get this supervisory position eighteen years ago. I was better than this other girl, everyone knew I was, and even the manager told me how hard I worked. But she deliberately undermined me by sleeping with him, and got to be the supervisor."

Unlike murder and assault, there is no DNA testing to be applied to undermining. Jill had no proof that the young woman in question was sleeping with her boss. Jill and the boss spoke frequently and laughed a lot together. Could she have also been told by the manager that she was a hard working assistant? Jill doubted that very much.

I said that there was no evidence that these two had been in a relationship – so let's talk about some other young lady who slept with her boss. Why did she do that? We are not excusing the behavior, it can have serious ramifications in the workplace, but let's just look at things from her point of view for a while.

There was hesitation. People empathize quite easily when they like or feel neutrally about someone. With people they dislike, it's more difficult. Once the women got started though, the conversation started to flow. We all came up with the following:

She was attracted to the boss.

She saw other people – or heard of other people doing it – and it jump-started their careers.

She was in genuine financial difficulties and sought the easy way out.

She was lazy and so decided to use her body.

She might have seen older people like us around who had never been promoted and did not want to be like us.

Me:	"Do you understand her somewhat better?"
The ladies:	"Yes, somewhat."
Me:	"Is your new manager sleeping with any-one?"
The ladies	"No."
Me:	" Do you understand how she must feel? Is this your reasoning – because a manager (supposedly) slept with a supervisor 15 years ago =I must punish the new manager for something that one did?

No, it wasn't only that, they said. This new manager thought too much of herself. I asked them: why are you letting that bother you? Three ladies could feel the new supervisor thinking (by her actions) *Here I am almost half your age and there you are in this junior position…How great I am – how low you are.*

We arrived at the conclusion that you encourage people to think of you by the way you project yourself. Isn't it difficult for many others to see us as better persons than we see ourselves? The ladies in question interestingly gave me quite a few examples where they knew this to be true. They however had only an intellectual understanding of that knowledge because they had not applied it to themselves.

But there was more, they said. This manager was a bully. She was very stern about the work. I asked – is being stern about the work an act of bullying? They again hesitated. Using probing questions, I discovered that the supervisor was not abusive. She was insistent that the work be done in concert with company policies. In their dislike of a new young manager, insistent instructions about how the work should be correctly done, had became bullying. At the end of two sessions, three admitted it was possible that their treatment of her was a consequence of what had previously happened in their work lives at the company.

Of that group of four, one modified her attitude, stayed, and was promoted to the position of supervisor only eight months later, and another was promoted to senior sales assistant. The other two stuck around until they were made redundant, but while they still worked at the store they did not make life as untenable for the supervisor, though now and then one had to be reminded to be a bit more cooperative. One of those who "stuck around" met me at the shopping plaza in which the store was located and thanked me for making a difference in her life. I was surprised.

She suggested she never stopped being a little bitter, but I had taken some of the anger out of her. She decided to really concentrate on her church mission.

I do not know what happened to the fourth one. Many people improve their attitudes and job prospects after redundancy, and I hope that was what happened. The manager did not leave, and continued to do an excellent job. So whereas the conflict was not "solved", it was "improved" and "improvement" is a far cry from doing nothing at all.

Having someone confidential with whom we can share concerns is a wonderful exhalation to the vast majority of employees. But having a confidential listener is only one critical aspect of health, and the following chapter discusses several components of a health program.

Case 3 – Persons who threaten physical violence – empty threats or not?

I inform anyone that if I hear a threat of physical violence or sabotage of the company's property that I must report it to management, so do not expect me to be confidential under these circumstances. This is the same kind of precaution that professional therapists and mediators take with respect to planned physical violence, child or elder abuse.

Body language alerts helping professionals that there may be an underlying anger problem. Since one of my gifts is that I am generally trusted, people often share with me whether their anger problems are home-related, work-related or both. A lot of anger is a complete waste of time and energy – most people would be surprised at the high number of conflicts that can be resolved quite easily. Misconceptions reign – managers won't listen, or I'm being victimized here. I invite employees to share these concerns with management, but I accompany them so that they feel safe, and then they find that these concerns are either resolved or abated. One case was a man, Tim, who asserted that he and his fellow workers threatened to "do something" to their supervisor because the supervisor had arranged for their coworker to be fired. Actually, the organization had discovered that the coworker had been stealing and had let him go confidentially to protect the supervisor – but the coworker had informed his friends that his termination was due to "victimization".

It is noteworthy that theft in that particular organization was not considered a crime to a robust percentage of the non-supervisory employees in a particular department – they upgraded the concept of theft to the constructive effort of "helping themselves" to augment their low salaries. The organization decided to expose the reason why the worker was fired, offering *evidence*. When the worker and his colleagues also understood why the supervisor would have been easily exposed and fired for retaining known thieves, they worked reasonably well with the supervisor until that supervisor left the company several years later for a management position elsewhere.

CHAPTER 6

A Health Program for Conflict Prevention and Management

The World Health Organization (WHO) defined health as far back as 1948 as "a state of complete physical, mental and social well-being and not merely the absence of disease or infirmity.[101] Because happiness is a fundamental goal of human existence, WHO increasingly emphasizes that happiness is a component of health. It is debatable whether workplaces are to provide for the general happiness of employees. However, having the systems and procedures that encourage employees to become fully engaged in their work and not overly stressed, is probably a form of happiness.

Unmanaged stress is a common precursor to the bullying, undermining and physical violence which lead to greater stress. Chronic stress is both prevented and alleviated by well executed health or wellness[102] programs. Managers responsible for employee health may wish to incorporate all or some of the elements of the health program discussed in this chapter.

Pain and Discomfort Management

Employees with medical conditions (diabetes, heart conditions, HIV and so on) are often among the most talented. Whereas some individuals maintain their composure whilst in physical pain or discomfort, others simply cannot. If physical discomfort is compounded with other serious work problems, we are not at our best. Chronic migraines make us irritable and serious sinus problems render us phlegmatic.

Physical discomfort appeared to be a reason why 'Sally', a forty-five year old manager, shouted at employees in the presence of their colleagues, after which she would congratulate herself on her no-nonsense stance toward people and life in general. A colleague said this:

> "Sally has some wonderful ways when you really get to know her but she's awful when she's wound up. I couldn't work with her. She shouted angrily at everybody whether she liked them or not."

Talented employees refused to put up with Sally's instability, and resigned. Sally seemed untouchable, but was perceived as a liability when she was gratuitously unpleasant to a powerful executive. She was subsequently uninvited to executive meetings at the head office.

Sally and her allies fought in the undermining arena, revealing true or doctored salacious secrets for their new enemies. Sally also hurt the company by being offensive to union leaders during their annual negotiations.

A health check from a nurse revealed that Sally's blood pressure was particularly high. One could ask if Sally's disposition contributed to the high blood pressure or if her unique physical make up (including but not limited to her high blood pressure) contributed to her behavior, hard to say in such a chicken and egg case. The nurse insisted that Sally take action to improve her health to try and reduce the blood pressure and associated headaches. When Sally took appropriate medication and made important lifestyle changes, she did not slip into as many dark moods. She also took steps to get the kind of education to help move her into a more fulfilling career. Sally's physical *and* emotional health had improved.

Organizations that require employees over forty to have annual check ups clearly know what they are doing. Organizations that sensitize their employees to the benefits of visiting health care providers who are certified or knowledgeable in pain management are giving their people a bonus.

Nutrition

Sally introduced more fruits, vegetables and other nutritious foods into her diet. Foods affect blood pressure – for example, studies attest to the beneficial role of Omega 3 oils in reducing high blood pressure.[103] Rigorous research has indicated that whereas groups placed in stressful situations did not necessarily eat more, they tended to eat more *unhealthy* foods, and unhealthy foods tend to be more stress-creating.[104]

Nutrition and behavior is a multi-disciplinary area which is gathering a great deal of interest.

Studies have shown significant correlations between nutrition and violence.[105] For instance, a famous UK study found that adding vitamins, minerals and other nutritional elements to the diets of young offenders held in custody led to a 26% reduction in criminal and anti-social behaviors. "We tend to forget that humans are physical as well as psychological beings, and putting poor fuel into the brain seems significantly to affect social behavior" said the lead author of the study, Bernard Gesch.[106] Interestingly, Gesch's study was replicated in the Netherlands, where violence and aggression declined 34% among the group given supplements.[107]

Notably, though supplements were prescribed in this study, well-meaning persons often "prescribe" vitamins and minerals far exceeding the recommended daily allowances, possibly overtaxing the liver and kidney.[108] If the organization wishes to promote good nutrition, it should engage a qualified nutritionist to talk about nutrition or direct employees to a university or national health website.

There are several other ways that organizations assist their people to learn about proper nutrition. Canteens can be beautified with pictures and bulletins of the healthiest foods. If an employee craves junk food, she would need to purchase it elsewhere. The good news is that most employees opt to eat healthier foods if they are available at work.

CHAPTER 6

Exercise

Sally's former tension and tiredness were two critical elements of mood, and off-moods that reduce the likelihood of an individual exercising. We've known about the general benefits of exercise for a long time. The famous quote *"mens sana in corpore sano"*, which means "a healthy mind is in a healthy body" was stated by the Roman writer Juvenal in the first century A.D. Even before that, the philosopher Seneca was prescribing exercise as a way to achieve physical and mental health. There are happily a number of recent studies that associate exercise with a multitude of health benefits, including improved moods.[109] A long steady walk, for example, is known to improve moods.[110] [111]

Reports indicate that more than 40% of adults do not engage in recommended amounts of physical activity, citing time and money constraints, lack of motivation and problems pertaining to access to training facilities.[112] Employees may adhere to an exercise program when they learn that the signs of physical degeneration such as slumped shoulders, sagging skin, loss of vitality, stiff joints, weakness, and fatigue, although inevitable, are slowed by exercise.[113]

An exercise program should fit the individual's goals, age, and health status. Organizations that have gyms for employees should ideally engage a trained physical education professional, one who would counter not only under-enthusiasm, but over-enthusiasm. An exercise-addict strains her body, and may damage her musculoskeletal system. Twenty minutes of vigorous exercise per day three or four times per week is enough for most people.

The gentler forms of yoga and other non-aerobic exercise are more suitable for other individuals.

Meditation – mindfulness

Meditation involves allowing any thought or sensation to surface while maintaining a specific attentional stance: awareness is that of an attentive and non-attached observer without judgment or analysis.[114] Mindfulness uses the whole mind to observe the emotions at work without being overpowered by the emotions or denying their existence. In other words, it cleans up the inner frustration and turmoil which affects health, violence and intelligence.

The impact of mindfulness on health is clear. A nine year controlled clinical trial has shown that patients who practice transcendental meditation (TM) have reduced heart attack, stroke and death risks by 47% compared to those who did not engage in TM practices. In addition, significant reductions in psychological stress were found in the high-stress subgroup.[115]

The known benefits of meditation to counter violent tendencies are not new. Even from the 1980s, there was also a growing body of research to suggest that TM was beneficial to inmates in terms of reduced aggressive actions, and decreased recidivism. Research using sophisticated methods has shown that the collective practice of the more powerful Transcendental Meditation programs by about one percent of a society's population, produces an influence of harmony for the entire population in terms of decreased auto accidents, violence, and decrease in lost work days due to industrial action.[116]

Protective Benefits from Transcendental Meditation[117]

KNOWN RISK FACTORS	PROTECTIVE BENEFITS
Heart disease and stroke	Reduced heart disease and stroke
High levels of stress	Reduced levels of stress
Anti-social personality	Increased sensitivity to feelings of others, reduced hostility
High impulsivity	Reduced impulsivity
Earlier than usual risk taking behaviors, including drugs and alcohol	Reduced use of alcohol and non-prescription drugs
Low self regard	Higher self regard
Dishonesty	Greater regard for ethical behavior

Meditation impacts positively on intelligence. Shapiro and his colleagues found that meditation appears to result in improvements in intelligence, learning ability, and short and long term recall.[118] In another study, 56 undergraduates were randomly assigned to a meditation or non-meditation group. The intervention included a 1-hour session twice a week for an academic semester. The meditation group was instructed to meditate before and after studying and before exams. The experimental group enjoyed significantly higher grades than the control group.[119]

If it is now clear that meditation plays a major role in promoting emotional health and reducing stress, it is notable that a survey of over 600 people from three different organizations revealed that approximately 25% of the employees cited interpersonal stress as the worst job stressor.[120] Appropriate culture change in tandem with non-traditional methods like TM will clean up much interpersonal stress.

Sleep and Rest

Daily meditation promotes better quality sleep, since the body has been given the opportunity to deeply relax. Lack of quality sleep is a major contributor to burnout, which has several symptoms, including but not limited to a compulsion to work harder and neglect other important needs.[121]   Many studies illuminate the difficulties faced by people who do not receive adequate sleep,[122] and a most telling case comes from the study of battle. A battalion was divided into four groups, and then conducted fire missions every waking hour for 20 days straight. Four groups were divided by the amount of sleep: groups received seven hours, six hours, five hours and four hours of sleep. At the end of 20 days, the group that received 7 hours sleep fired at 98% efficiently, the group that got 6 hours sleep fired at 50% and Groups 3 and 4 fired at 28% and 15% respectively.[123]

What implications this study has for the decisions made by sleep-deprived leaders! As seen in the case where an executive, 'Len', protected a manager who bullied others with such freedom that three able and motivated employees left within two months. Len said "Well, if we look at the positive, we'll see we are getting in new blood." He was too tired to fully understand that his least productive employees were still in the system while his most productive employees had resigned. Len was burnt out, not only through overwork but lack of sleep. Just after he returned from vacation, he was rested enough to have full discussions with his coach. Before he got his landfall of sleep, it was difficult to reason with him.

Large-sample surveys have suggested that between 13% and 52% of those surveyed report at least occasional problems with insomnia. Although bouts of insomnia from time to time are probably of little long-term consequence, chronic insomnia has been found to correlate with physical discomfort, physical disability, and symptoms of social and emotional distress (Hamilton and colleagues, 2007).[124] More recent work has documented the effects of sleep loss in "higher level" cognitive tasks, such as those requiring creative problem solving, judgment, and decision making. [125]

It behooves the organization to discover those persons affected by chronic and severe sleep problems. A rich organization will be

able to engage a sleep specialist as a consultant. Other organizations should let their people know where they can go for help.

Emotional Intelligence

The best managers are usually the most adult in their behavior, and certainly would not use undermining or bullying as strategies. They are called wise, emotionally healthy, balanced or emotionally intelligent. Daniel Goleman defines emotional intelligence (EI) as "the capacity for recognizing our own feelings and those of others, for motivating ourselves, and for managing emotions well in our-selves and our relationships". [126]

EI, which is essentially best-practice thinking and behavior, has been a popular concept in management since Goleman's first book on the subject,[127] and has become even more popular since it has been associated with productivity. Goleman's research found that performers with EI are 127% to 1272% more productive than average performers. The best performing sales clerks are 12 times more productive than the least competent and 85% more productive than the average sales clerk. Approximately one-third of the difference is due to skills and ability while two-thirds is due to EI. Many other instances of research on emotional intelligent competences also point to economic benefits.[128]

Proactivity and reactivity are viewed as emotionally intelligent depending on culture. There are important culturally related differences in EI. For example, it is likely that Indians may function better with a more directive, task-oriented style of leadership, rather than a participative style characteristic of most U.S. managers. The power distances in countries like India and other Asian cultures are higher, and employers will encourage their employees to be followers and more reactive than proactive. Western societies with relatively low power differences will assume that their employees will want to be more proactive and participatory. [129]

EI practices should be highlighted in meetings addressing areas such as customer care, promotion of the company's goods and products, environmental health and occupational safety. Regular articles about EI can be placed in the company's newsletter or on employee information boards, giving illustrations of best practice. Consider the following:

The Hay Group states that a study of 44 Fortune 500 companies demonstrate that salespersons with high EI were able to produce double the revenue of those with average or below average scores.

Hallmark Communities sales staff who developed EI were 25% more productive than their low EQ[130] counterparts and EQ was more important to executive job performance than character, strategic thinking, and focus on results. TalentSmart's EQ learning program raised individual and team EQ for the low and high EQ groups to improve group cohesion and job performance.

Coca Cola saw division leaders who developed EQ competencies outperform their targets by more than 15%. Division leaders who didn't develop their EQ missed targets by the same margin.

A multinational consulting firm measured the EQ of senior partners on EI competencies. Partners high in EQ were responsible for $1.2 million more profit each in their clients than low EQ partners. High EQ partners showed a 139% gain in profit.[131]

Forgiveness

An aspect of EI would be the ability to forgive. One of the most satisfying things we hear of is persons forgiving each other for serious breaches of humanity. The high level of divorces in western societies suggests either a general difficulty in forgiving or a general non-willingness to put up with certain things that affront one's dignity.

Forgiving is clearly easier in some contexts than others. A relative alerted me to the fact that an acquaintance who had once spoken well about the importance of forgiveness was now in a situation where he was not forgiving a colleague even after an extended period of time. I told my relative that his acquaintance might have been able to forgive what had been done to him previously but the new "breach" was not something he might have considered ever happening to himself. It is easier to forgive someone who has done something particularly hurtful to you in the past, than someone who continues to do the distressing act. We also tend to be more forgiving if and when we get our lives back in order.

Bullying, undermining and physical violence would be material for forgiveness. Forgiveness of course in the workplace and other aspects of life can be quite different. In our regular lives, we may forgive someone but avoid them at all costs because we know that they have grave character faults. In a toxic workplace, we rarely escape interacting with these individuals whose moral courage has been seriously debilitated.

Forgiveness takes time, and in particularly tough cases, it is usually attached in some form of atonement from the offender. Forgiveness is not always appropriate. Not everyone who bullies, for example, is going to cease bullying someone who has adopted a forgiving approach – an astute and emotionally damaged perpetrator will exploit the target even further.

An integrated conflict management program, recommended in Chapter 2, will serve to unravel the majority of conflicts to the point of no-retaliation, or acceptance. At times, there will be reconciliation, which is the advanced form of forgiveness. Tavuchis states that there has not been much work on the social and psycho-dynamic sources of forgiveness, and that there should be a sociology of forgiveness.[132] But the area certainly isn't only academic or simply a discussion of what other persons have forgiven.[133] If a forgiveness specialist is engaged, it is helpful that he only relate cases of how others have been able to forgive egregious acts, but reveal something very real and significant that *he* has forgiven. He should also discuss the process, and whether or not reconciliation was appropriate in the circumstances.

Spiritual Health

Forgiveness is the living room in the mansion of spiritual health. Other rooms contain love, caring, wisdom, imagination and compassion. Indeed, spiritual health is expressed in a myriad of ways, including interactions characterized by love, trust, integrity, and sacrifice.

We know that religion and spirituality are protective factors for young people.[134] Where both young people and older adults are concerned, in a meta-analysis of data over a period of 30 years, Baier and Wright concluded that there was a modest protective effect of religious beliefs and participation on overtly criminal behavior, but there was no consistent definition of either criminality or religiousness in the situations they investigated.[135] [136]

A rich inner spirit, difficult to precisely define, and spirituality, takes on different forms in different individuals. I know of a lady of 75, overweight by about 50 pounds, but whose first significant health problem was having intermittent high blood pressure a couple of years ago. She has very close friends, eats a healthy diet, yet hardly exercises. With such a healthy spirit, she has far fewer health and mental problems than some of her acquaintances who adhere to every single healthy practice. Genes might also be at play here.

People with a rich inner spirit tend to find humor in challenging circumstances and can laugh at themselves. Studies show that laughter may have health benefits, even pain-reducing benefits such as helping the pituitary gland to release pain-suppressing opiates.[137] People of the bountiful garden seem to carry a suitcase of beautiful emotions such as gratitude which they can open at almost any occasion. They are remarkably resilient.

True emotional health is about the kind of strength that benefits both the employee and the organization. It is true coping, the mental six-pack associated with resilience. Once an individual becomes tough and experiences the sustained energy (with minimal tension) necessary for successful coping, that person is likely to think of unusual experiences as challenging rather than threatening. That combination of optimism and energy should lead to the successes that stimulate more optimism and the acceptance of more challenges.

Happy people are not technically "whole." There are elements of denial, elements of dysfunction in everyone, but happy people are able to adapt to change faster. They are not unrealistic, but know how to address obstacles, and they discover opportunities where others fixate on obstacles.

The Individual in the Community

We do not need to live in a caring community to have a rich, inner spirit, but it helps, as suggested in this quote from Malcolm Gladwell's book *Outliers.*

"The results were astonishing. In Roseto, virtually no one under fifty-five had died of a heart attack or showed any signs of heart disease. For men over sixty-five, the death rate from heart disease in Roseto was roughly half that of the United States as a whole. The death rate from all causes in Roseto, in fact, was 30 to 35 percent lower than expected."

In Roseto, 41% of the calories of the residents came from fat, which no responsible physician would approve of, and other aspects of their diet would not have been considered healthy by modern day standards. In addition, there was no strong genetic link: cousins who migrated from Roseto to other areas of the United States did not share the same good health. The verdict was that the community was engaged in activities that forged and maintained a close link.[138]

The organization can do little about the communities in which their employees live, unless it is the major force within that particular community. The organization can only encourage employees to be active in its community outreach programs, or their own communities.[139] Community participation will also enhance the organization's corporate reputation in the community at large, in addition to strengthening team work, honing talents, and allowing employees to be recognized for other fulfilling tasks other than work.

Acceptance of Different Others

A form of "global health" is the acceptance of others who are, or are perceived to be different. Here I talk about people from other cultures and highly creative people.

One of my best friends was born in Guangdung, China. Because she has invited me into her life and her family, I have discerned some aspects of life in her region of China. China of course is a country with a multitude of sub-cultures and perspectives. There is a respect in many provinces for a Confucius-like spirit, where the world is viewed through the eyes of harmony. They may even say they do not experience conflict. A person born in the west without the appropriate understanding of persons with different cultures might cry "denial" and "conflict-avoidance". If the person migrates to the West, he may be now pressured to see the Western perspective. The truth is that there *may* be some elements of denial contained within a harmonious way of seeing life, but not to the extent that the Western trained mind might see it.

It is easier to accept persons like oneself: whether they are of the same nationality, race, religion and so on. Accepting others perceived to be very different from oneself, is a potentially huge and interesting field. It is the reduction of the "who on earth are you?" to "who are you?" The aim is to judge a person on their *character* and not on their otherness.

Highly creative persons come from another country in the figurative sense. Highly creative people who may not be able to adhere to strictly developed emotional intelligence, as suggested by Csikszentmihalyi & Csikszentmihalyi:

"Emotional intelligence involves being attuned to social norms and complying with what most people find acceptable …highly creative people often exhibit behaviors and traits that distinguish them from their peers…these individuals tend to be more emotionally sensitive, anxious, emotionally liable, and impulsive than other people…work on emotional creativity has shown that the ability to experience unusual or novel emotional experiences might aid the creative process. Being acutely attuned to social norms may hinder the ability to experience such novelty. Therefore, creative expression is a domain in which being emotionally intelligent might not be a helpful attribute." [140] (Csikszentmihalyi & Csikszentmihalyi 2006 p. 115)

Highly creative people are different in an important way, such as being particularly humorous, recalcitrant, or defiant. Because they bring something different to the table, they may be able to inspire others to reach significant heights. Organizations might topple over themselves to get hold of a creative marketing genius, in the way that a top baseball team will go after the best talent. All of the greatest innovations have been made by highly creative persons.

Highly creative persons often work best alone. Astute executives might arrange for highly creative persons to work essentially alone if needed and also to create other kinds of situations that would allow that level of innovativeness to flow.[141] I have heard a highly innovative person accuse his colleague of being essentially a carbon copy of everyone else, while the "carbon copy" confronted his accuser of being "mad". There does seem to be some sort of divergency in the brains of highly creative people, however, bizarre behavior does not automatically suggest creative genius.[142] Moreover, a balance is required, and a highly creative person with the attitude of *I'm creative – so accept me whatever I do* would be counterproductive.

If persons from various cultures (including the highly divergent culture of creativity) are employed, the training department should at least conduct an annual or biannual sensitization program for its executives, managers and supervisors on how to communicate with others who are or who are perceived to be very different to themselves.

Inspirers for Health

Every company needs a cadre of intelligent inspirers who have the gift of helping others to create satisfying futures for themselves. Inspirers create other inspirers. Inspirers usually like to inspire in their "pet" areas but thankfully many are attracted to the area of positive interpersonal relationships and health. If they can be reminded of strong advantages of inspiring a large number of colleagues, and understand the few downsides of "inspiration",[143] they're ready to go.

Who are the company's inspirers? Everyone in the company may know already. If not, employees could be given the opportunity to confidentially select their top inspirers from a list of the staff complement. Identifying who are perceived as inspirers will let management know a great deal about the organizational culture. But it is more than just identifying true inspirers. Inspirers need to be managed effectively to create the impact both they and the company want. They too will need to know what is expected of them, and how they will be rewarded by their efforts, either monetarily or otherwise. The leaders would then choose inspirers, ideally those who have a record of good performance.

The purpose of a campaign is to launch a particular concept. Wellness campaigns are important, especially for companies that have a non-existent or moderate wellness program. It has been shown that environmental organizations have won support for sustainability through campaigns, and the campaign allies itself well with conflict management. A campaign is a most creative activity and may include activities such as talks, posters, fairs, demonstrations and displays. Employees normally enjoy getting involved in any campaign that deals with the reduction of stress. The campaign should, like virtually every other major tool promoting change, be endorsed by the CEO and other executives.

Campaign leaders should advise how healthy behavior will be maintained or reinforced after the campaign has ended. The real work actually begins after the campaign – the campaign is essentially a public relations tool. Campaign-leaders get a boost when they are praised for their efforts in helping colleagues to enhance or maintain their physical and emotional health.

CHAPTER 7

A Single Manager's Influence

The difficulties lie, not in the new ideas, but in escaping from the old ones, which ramify, for those brought up as most of us have been, into every corner of our minds.

John Maynard Keynes

Happily, history and the present day provide us with countless examples of individuals who have initiated positive change in very difficult situations, who have believed in people when no one else or few others did. It is not only Ghandi, Mandela and others who transform entire nations. If one person, Marva Collins, could encourage students in inner cities to accomplish feats of scholarly achievement, even students considered to be intellectually challenged - then one manager can be powerful indeed.

Sometimes a single manager works in an organization that cannot afford to go through expansive culture change. It is very difficult for him to take on an entire large or middle sized organization: as I have previously stated, single execution rarely works in such situations. He does what he can to create a partial oasis in his *own* department. If the organization is not hostility-ridden and he is an astute and clear communicator, he can influence his seniors, colleagues and team to see things his way, such as 'Dave' did.

Dave carved a partial oasis for himself and his team. He had inherited a messy warehouse operational system and the conflicted triad – undermining, bullying and physical violence. Within a year, Dave reduced loss in the large warehouse to less than 60% of the previous manager. He told me that handling conflicts effectively was an important factor in that reduced loss, explaining that unresolved conflicts hampered productivity. He said: "Every month I'm still aware of conflicts that could crop up – I either deal with actual conflicts or try to prevent them …even with this (improved) team." Dave was disciplined enough to commit to the change, even when a bit frustrated, adhering to Jim Rohn's quotation "for every disciplined effort there is multiple reward."

Judgment, the Foundation to Steady the Steps

The manager with influence learns the layers of the culture and the unwritten rules. So if she is breaking rules, she knows, and forges a strategy to deflect the protracted disharmony that may weaken her position within the organization.

Tichy and Warren state that "the most successful leaders make a high percentage of successful judgment calls when it counts the most".[144] A manager can make those successful judgment calls regardless of leadership style, or culture. In some national and organizational cultures, employees are simply required to get work completed by a certain time, and need to find ways to address their conflicts themselves, because if they don't produce, they're out. Other cultures adopt a somewhat gentler approach, where employees are helped to exercise good judgment with respect to resolving conflicts.

Experience facilitates good judgment, but the process of learning superior judgment also suggests the finding of relevant career-related information to digest, in addition to those add-on fields that are so necessary to understand to work in a healthy workplace. For example, managers whose departments have a history of physical or verbal violence may not receive the opportunity to attend seminars or courses. They should read literature on improving interpersonal relationships and workplace violence prevention, or consult persons knowledgeable in those fields. By investigating the effects of bullying, managers and team members could write a one-page departmental "newsletter", which is either given to each person or posted on the notice board. To eliminate or reduce undermining, departmental managers may state in meetings which kind of communication behaviors they approve of, and those that they do not support.

Managers will not be able to do much learning during tradition-ally hectic periods like the end of the financial year, but the manager who can never slow down, who is in a constant stage of agitation, will experience burnout, and make errors in judgment.

Where to Start:
The Manager's Personal Vision Statement and Philosophy Towards Conflict Prevention and Resolution

The manager establishes his own values as the first step. A colleague of mine, who completed a character strengths survey, found that curiosity was his number one value. This surprised him, because he had never considered "curiosity" to be a value.[145] He subsequently forged a personal and professional strategy which would make use of this value instead of trying to use values antithetical to his nature. He enjoyed working on his plan for the first time, because it was closely and creatively allied to his vision and values.

After developing a professional vision statement, the manager determines how he monitors anything that is not easy for him. If it is conflict, he learns more than the steps for resolution - he learns how to use his personal values to help him resolve conflicts. But values are not only positive. If the manager values the enjoyment and power derived from bullying the team members he does not like, he should determine if his need to punish ends as a punishment to self, in terms of the backlash that it often brings. He would also see if he is incurring unconstructive tension by openly keeping favorites.

Managers can sometimes craft their jobs to be in tune with their strongest values. A job can be crafted by enriching or expanding a job, allowing the managers to mold their jobs to fit their strongest performance traits. For example, a sales manager could craft his job by spending a bit more time than average branding the product to employees, their families and friends. [146]

The Management of Liking Somebody More

It is difficult for the majority of us not to like some of our colleagues more than others. We are generally attracted to persons who perform at a high level, keep their promises, are able to keep classified information confidential, or who are wise and compassionate persons. Clearly, however, some discretion is required especially when others may harm the ones we like or respect so much. In the Bible, Jacob's favoritism of Joseph motivated Joseph's brothers to sell him into slavery. Favoritism has the potential for creating unhappiness within a department as much as in a family. Here I am talking about real favoritism associated with special benefits or *perceived* special benefits. It is unlikely that reasonable employees will mind if a manager likes one of their colleagues a bit more, or gives extra remuneration or other awards to colleagues clearly superior in work quality or output.

Managers should ask themselves the following questions:

1. Do I openly have favorites – and is it because these favorites are excellent workers or some other reason?

2. How does having open favorites affect others in the department or company?

3. Do others feel as though they are justified in undermining my favorites?

4. Has favoritism affected the favored one? Is she abrasive to her colleagues, or does she work well with them?

5. Is my behavior significantly different toward the favored ones and the unfavored – for example, am I consistent with my favorites, but when I say something to the others, they are actually guessing what I'll say or do next?

A manager may consider work untenable without a cadre of favorites (aka loyalists), believing that this is the only way to survive or thrive at work. But open favoritism, especially to an employee of average or below-average performance, means that negative politics has entered the veins of the departmental culture. Incompetence can be negotiated for loyalty – I see your general incompetence, you give me your support in exchange for your incompetence and I'll protect you. Actually, unrepentant incompetence in itself is a form of disloyalty, whether unintended or not, because it creates more work for the manager and his department. It also makes undermining appear more justified – in other words, employees tend to not feel guilty undermining a manager who keeps an incompetent favorite.

There are managers who simply do not keep favorites. A manager I knew, 'Bill', hired his girlfriend and expected her to work above the standard of the other employees. Bill said "If she feels she can do bad work because of our relationship, then we have to break up, because she is not the person I would have wanted to be with in the first place."

I once related this story to a manager who was also my friend. He said "He's too good, my girlfriend would *kill* me." Even if not everyone can be as "perfect" as Bill, having a flagrantly open cadre of loyalists goes along with having a cadre of silent "disloyalists". Perpetrators of violence almost always consider themselves unfavored before committing the violence. Even if the manager is not likely to have violent team members, he can unwittingly harbour a team of Those Rendered Cynical, who undermine their managers on a daily basis. Managers who refuse to be targets but do not have sufficient conflict management skills at their disposal will bully their resident cynics, thereby allowing dysfunctional boils to fester in their departments.

Indeed, the management of dislike is a most critical life skill.

The Management of Dislike

Managers may dislike one or more team members for a variety of reasons, but the individuals with whom managers have most problems are the incompetent, the undependable and the cynical. The undependable and the incompetent can usually be helped through coaching and good performance assessment systems. Cynics are more challenging to deal with.

Former President Lyndon B Johnson once said "If one morning I walked on top of the water across the Potomac River, the headline that afternoon would read PRESIDENT CAN'T SWIM. That headline would have been written by a cynic, whose memories have been justifiably or unjustifiably tainted with chronic disappointment in the behavior of his fellow human beings. The cynic retains distrust of the organization or manager for historical reasons, perhaps for such a long period that the cynic does not even remember how to work in a positive environment.

Because "cynicism" is politically incorrect, cynics often call themselves skeptical, which means doubting an assertion based on instinct or previous experience but without the sting of acrimony associated with cynicism. Without the armor of acrimony, a cynic can feel naked and vulnerable. That being said, it is difficult *not* to be a cynic in chronically dysfunctional organizations. These organizations have beaten cynicism into otherwise reasonable individuals, because every plan for significant improvement has not been realized. The open cynic is often the most honest person in the department saying directly what the less-brave mumble about. It is this level of honesty that can be disconcerting to some managers.

Managers are often more upset with the open cynics, not realizing that she may have among her team many cynics in the closet. Closet cynics either say nothing, or even say positive things about the manager or organization to the faces of the persons who have influence over their salary cheque. Their cynicism is apparent in the fact that they take two days to complete a critically important report when they had the opportunity and skills to easily do so in four hours. Closet cynics can be the most proficient of under-miners. To help closet cynics to grow into vibrant team members, good communication and team work are needed, discussed later in this chapter.

Managers have told me even though they do not like the idea of team members saying bad things behind their back, the fact that they do not do so *in front* of their faces shows a measure of respect. Managers feel harassed by open cynics especially when it is difficult to transfer or fire them. Open cynics introduce doubt in each possible aperture in their communication with the team, and damn with faint praise anything that might actually work well. Sometimes open cynics only express their doubts by their bodily expressions at a meeting but fill everyone's heads at the lunch table on why that idea that the manager was talking about was rubbish – a conversation which they may actually hope gets back to the manager in one form or another, in order for the manager to understand the real power dynamics in that organization. Yes, intelligent hard core cynics can have the most real power in the organization, more than any "legitimate" power figure in the department! Open cynics are usually comfortable in the fact that they are difficult to fire for some reason or another, and after any delicious hint of managerial injustice, finds himself at the door of the union leader forthwith.

If the manager is concerned about being embarrassed by an open cynic's comments in a meeting, she should discuss issues with the cynic on a one and one basis in her office or in a meeting room. This of course depends on the integrity of the particular individual. Witnesses will be needed for the individual who will blissfully misquote the manager upon leaving her office.

The perceptive manager ensures that her own behavior has not helped to fuel that cynicism. She does the homework to ensure that her ideas have a good possibility of working, and avoid speaking in 100 percents: that is, it is a certainty that what I say will come true. She allies the goal achievement to her own competence and the competence and willingness of the group. She prepares for negative remarks and to reply to them in a wise and calm manner. She speaks naturally, avoiding the management jargon that fuels cynicism. If she feels that she will be trapped by a particularly clever cynic, she should arm herself with knowledge of informal logic.[147]

If humility is required to successfully communicate with most intelligent employees, it is particularly true when communicating with the cynic, who is almost always highly intelligent. The manager's humility precludes cynics and other listeners having loud conversations inside their heads in reaction to a wonderful thing the manager just said about herself. These conversations are usually so loud so as to drum out their listening to the parts of the presentation that have to do with work.

Here are some responses to some of the more common assertions of cynics. The tone of voice used to the cynic is paramount – assertive and respectful with no tint of sarcasm:

CYNIC	MANAGER
This company can't improve.	The company must offer you some benefits for you to have worked here for so long. None of us would stay in a company that simply couldn't improve. In that light, what can you do to help the company?
This can't work.	How would you make it work? (Yes, I know you are not paid to

	make it work, but if you were, how would you proceed?)
	What would you do? What are the strengths and limitations to your decisions, if you were to think like a business owner (or executive)?
We're always doing new things.	Did they all not work, why didn't they, and what can you personally do to help?

In each case the cynic is asked to help, and the manager can suggest ways if he does not know how to. Even cynics begin to become convinced that something is working once they see improvements. They can even become the strongest allies of the manager. But in cases where a diehard cynic continues to damage the good spirits in a department or company, I recommend that the manager use her political acumen to pave the way for the cynic to leave the organization with dignity. Excellent organizations retain the dictum that if an employee cannot work with the organization's values, he should leave, regardless of the level of his competencies. The multiplier effect of negative behaviors is simply too great.

Avoiding the Translation of Hot Emotions into Undermining, Bullying and Physical Violence

Of course, anger is not only felt by cynics, but by the most reasonable of persons. And not all anger is bad - without anger the greatest changes of benefit to humankind would have never been realized.

Once a strong emotion is being felt but not being expressed, there is a hard conflict, which can express itself in undermining, bullying and physical violence. There is a relationship between thought suppression and stress intrusive thoughts (for example, anxiety and substance use), and attempts to suppress the thoughts could even precipitate an increase in those thoughts.[148]

Repressed thoughts leak into our behavior. One may, for example, find a supervisor who believes that she is communicating quite neutrally with her team, but who dresses provocatively and makes subtle come-ons to her male colleagues. Her team reacts to the behavior, not to the repression or what she says – so the outcome will be miscommunication. She will not be aware of what she is doing, yet others will think she is being deliberately seductive to men. It would be better if she were aware of her emotions, or admitted them – which is not always easy. A helping professional may be required to assist her. Matthieu Ricard in Goleman (2003) explains why expressing our emotions is cathartic:

"We don't have to suppress our emotions. We can channel them into a dialogue with our intelligence, using them to

142

understand the nature of our mind, watching how they subside of their own accord without creating more seeds for their future arising. For the moment, one thus avoids the harmful consequences of hatred, and in the long term, it will have no cause for reappearing in such violent ways." (p. 84-85) [149]

This includes identifying and slowly discarding the emotions that keep us in impasse, including our need to dislike, be angry, to be right, and to win. Our experience is not the sole source of truth even though it automatically allows us to formulate a position. When we understand that there are multiple truths operating, this allows us to shift our focus and identify interests.[150]

Tal Ben-Shahar states that although experiencing negative emotions is natural, it is not necessary to hold on to anger toward others for protracted periods of time. He recommends that our decision to reconcile or condemn should be assessed using happiness as the standard. He says "We need to ask ourselves the simple question with the complex answer: which path will lead to the highest profits in the ultimate currency?" Ben-Shahar recommends that we write down the price that we and the other persons are paying for the conflict. [151]

Clearly, the manager's positive and negative emotions are particularly contagious because she is the most important role sender in her department. If a manager's emotion changes from frustration to an active interest, the listener would still likely be reacting to the frustration communicated a few minutes ago. Fisher and Shapiro state that "the impact of a negative emotion lingers long after it has passed. The stronger and more troublesome the emotion, the greater the risk that both of you will lose control."[152]

Goleman and Boyatzis[153] state that if a manager laughs or frowns, similar behaviors will be evident among the team, and say that:

"Shared behaviors unify a team, and bonded groups perform better than fragmented ones...positive behaviors – such as exhibiting empathy – create a chemical connection between a leader's and his followers' brains. By managing these interconnections adroitly, leaders can deliver measurable business results. For example, after one executive at a *Fortune 500* company worked with a coach and role model to improve her behavior, employee retention and emotional commitment in her unit soared. And the unit's annual sales jumped 6%."

When the manager manages his own emotions with greater success, he is better able to ask what the emotions of others are really saying. The emotion could be saying, for example, "I am angry because I do not feel that you are respecting me." The manager diagnoses the emotion and reacts to its concern appropriately without becoming angry. He is more observant of the manner in which messages are expressed: the subtext, process, timing and speed. This kind of communication will also let the manager know if someone is being bullied, because targets tend to look worried or stressed-out.

A manager with this level of perceptivity becomes even more skilled at putting frames around other's communication. Sometimes I ask managers to think of a harmless looking picture of a calm ocean with a frame made of forks. The frame might make one think of the calm before the storm or vice versa. It is this frame that tells us how to interpret the meaning behind the words and determine whether they are innocuous or not. I ask the managers to listen to a number of statements framed by body language and tone, to see how able they were to ascertain what the person making the statement was actually feeling. With practice, they can become outstanding communicators.

The excellent communicator is also better at managing the differences among individuals and teams. Differences are what create "good conflict" and very few managers want the team to be programed in the innovation-deprived group-think mode. The able communicator does not, however, emphasize individuality and differences so strongly that cooperation is an afterthought. He senses when to best avoid a difference or conflict, or shape the difference into a clearly defined conflict (if conflict is vague and nebulous), or use the differences for constructive problem-solving. He is ready to be a consistently effective communicator to both new employees and those older in the system. He is clearly protecting himself and his team from undermining, bullying and violence.

A Conflict Prevention Strategy for New Employees

Tools and assessments like the Myers-Briggs Assessment tools, DISC, The Strong, and other excellent tools allow new employees to see how they work best in a variety of situations, to work with others who have different work personalities, and with the help of the manager, develop a positive way forward with no intractable conflicts. The human resource manager clearly explains the performance management system, and the department manager shares his philosophy, what he values in his team members and what he does not. Apart from emphasizing the need for good quality work, a manager in a department with a history of physical violence might wish to outline the company's policy on violence.

New employees of course require regular coaching and feedback. If this is not done, an organization can retain not-quite-effective employees for decades. That new employee who comes in looking fresh and enthusiastic could be a repository of bleak thoughts within a year. Which senior clerk after ten years in the accounting department is going to ask basic questions about the accounting policy and procedures he should have known years ago? He may think that someone might think him stupid to not have asked the question before – and in fairness to him, someone might.

The more immediate the reinforcement the new employee receives from his manager, the easier his work will be, and by extension, the manager's work. The perceptive manager holds a formal meeting for every new member of staff in a formal meeting before and after the first or second week of work. The manager and the new recruit are still two strangers, and need to get to know each other's work habits in a fuller way than the interview or recruitment system will allow. These meetings will permit the new recruit to grow out of best-face interview speak in a safe mode while learning how the manager leads and works.

The excellent manager takes time to discover talents, and discuss ways in which those talents can be used as well to engage the person at work. Examples of discussion topics are:

- What you do and do not appreciate at work (if they are reluctant to speak, give them examples).

- Tell me a conflict that you did not handle well. What would you do differently now?

An illustration of an assignment is:

- I'm going to give you a month to reflect and plan how you are going to incorporate the team's philosophy into your work.

New employees will forever remember this first talk – and assignment – perhaps far more than any other talk the manager will ever deliver. This initial sharing communication between strangers works.[154] If the manager does not have the time to personally train, there should be the appropriate delegation of training to a seasoned employee who is competent and is willing and able to coach. The trainer asks the new employee on a weekly basis to write down the 3-6 most important things they have learned within the first three or six months.

EMPLOYEES OLDER IN THE SYSTEM

There are instances where a good team philosophy is unspoken and the team performs well. Usually this is a team of intrinsically motivated, talented people who enjoy high levels of emotional intelligence to boot. Realistically, not every team fits into this easy headache-free paradigm. Most teams require articulated values to perform at their optimum. Perceptive managers should therefore share their philosophies about collaborative work effort with their teams, or ask the team to help extrapolate one constructive philosophy from their various viewpoints.

You hear employees say all the time "Mrs. James says so and so." Employees are very much aware of what their managers and supervisors say often. Employees must be aware of what their managers say to survive in the workplace. If they have a high respect for their managers, their managers' work philosophies tend to become theirs.

It is best for the team to have 1 to 3 core values, instead of the 12 that sound great and to which no one can live up to, partly because no one can remember all 12. If the values contain words as amorphous as 'respect' then the team can find two or three specific ways in which respect needs to be shown – and build on these ways in other meetings as time goes on. The effective manager relates important decisions to the team philosophy, or asks the team how they relate their decisions to the philosophy. If the department is prone to violent attacks, the team should be encouraged to make anti-violence as one of their team philosophies.

Apart from working with articulated philosophies and values, the creative manager introduces monthly or quarterly themes. One of the themes could be conflict prevention followed by another meeting addressing conflict management. A mistake managers make is addressing such themes one time only. One time only messages rarely work, and that is why marketers put on a series of advertisements in the media. Even after the manager changes the topic to something other than conflict management, she should put in a reminder about conflict management (or related topic) every now and then for maintenance.

By emphasizing good interpersonal relationships and by practicing them himself, the manager wins natural loyalty. He enjoys even more loyalty if he helps his team to solve problems, not only at work but in their careers generally. We all tend to be very loyal to those who want to see us progress in this world.

A Tool to Reduce Tension and Improve Operations

Unconstructive tension is usually mitigated when all team members know exactly what they ought to do. In today's environment, however, it is not always wise to specify which employees should do which tasks – teams need to do each other's jobs when required.

There are many tools that help to elicit team cooperation – the simple form on page 151 looks at operations and interpersonal relationships. The team shares in at least some of the decisions regarding the operations, and in all of the decisions regarding how they will work together. Strengths should be highlighted as well as opportunities for improvement.

The completed form highlights successes and audits and corrects the factors that prevent the achievement of departmental objectives. Past operations are related to present concerns, and to ascertain what beneficial procedures, systems and impactful inter-personal behaviors to retain and not to retain in the present. The form is reviewed weekly, monthly or quarterly as required.

The form can be used as is or tailored to suit the managers' style and operations. For example, the form need not have what it obtained in the past, but just focus on the present and the future. With tools such as these, and with a plan to improve judgment and communication, the manager influences her team and feels as though she is genuinely in charge of her department.

Indeed, there are a number of tools and techniques that managers can use to introduce fresh air into their departments. Managers who get their teams behind them certainly seem to enjoy their work far more than others. Whatever the manager decides to do, he and the team should have some enjoyment. The team that enjoys itself with its manager will have little use for undermining, bullying and violence, but will actively seek to achieve salubriousness and sanity.

Question	Operations Before this year (Optional) Note: This is to show the difference, and the new changes between structure, employee responsibilities, authorities and costs	Operations - Now	How the team works/communicates – (Before this year) Also note how team dealt with conflict in this box	How the team works/communicate– Now Note how team plans to deal with conflict in this box
What does this department need to do in relation to the overall strategic plan?				
What are key performance benchmarks for the department?				
Question	Operations Before this year (Optional) This is to show the difference, and the new changes between structure, employee responsibilities and costs	Operations – Now	What were the most important behaviors for success? (Before this year) Also note how team dealt with conflict in this box	What are the most important behaviors for success now? Note how team plans to deal with conflict in this box
What value does this job bring to the team?				
What are key performance benchmarks for success for this job?				

POSTSCRIPT

Most organizational conflict is not beneficial, but an enormous waste of time and resources. Conflict is a major reason why many large organizations do not have greater financial wealth, and why many other organizations lie in a stalemate or state of decline. Too many people do not share their best ideas in dysfunctional organizational cultures, too many people have their health compromised, and the most talented and emotionally intelligent leave while the others remain in a state or torpor or in the midst of thickening political games.

What is challenging is that an organization is always doing something well, and it is tempting to say "well, we have this great new product, so we're doing okay." We have seen that a company with a good product and location can still make a healthy profit and have unhealthy conflict within. It is both a business and an ethical choice to manage the conflict well.

It is a choice to respect the persons who work at all levels within the organization, which in turn helps employees to truly respect their leaders and their organizations. As seen in this book, conflict management is a system which involves culture modification, values that promote both the health of the organization and the health of the individuals, relevant and effective learning programs, ensuring the availability of a trustworthy person with whom organizational citizens can share their conflicts, and the empowerment of individual managers. Managing conflict well is one of the characteristics of the strong manager, and can lead to other positive developments. In democratic societies, in which we are born with the entitlement to liberty, the empowerment of managers will lead to the empowerment of the business and not-for-profit organization.

References and Notes

INTRODUCTION

[1]   Influenced by E. Van de Vliert (1985) "Escalative Intervention in Small-Group Conflicts" *Journal of Applied Behavioral Science*, pp. 19-36.

[2]   The case of a Motorola business which shows reductions in disputes – cases involving conflicts declined as sales increased from 1986-1990. From Stucki, Hans U (1996) "Measuring the Merit of ADR." 14 *Alternatives* 90 (CPR Institute for Dispute Resolution, July 1996).

CHAPTER 1

[3]   In a workplace violence study conducted by Thomas Staffing Services in California, the HR executives least likely to be concerned about violence in the workplace were those who (naively) claimed to "never have had a problem" with it. Schell, B. H. & Lanteigne, N. M. (2000) Westport, CT: *Stalking,*

Harassment, and Murder in the Workplace: Guidelines for Protection and Prevention Quorum Books, 2000. p. 52.

[4] Ekman, P. (2002) *Telling Lies: Clues to Deceit in the Marketplace, Politics, and Marriage.* New York: W.W. Norton & Company. Page 23.

[5] Peters, T. "Just Say Yes!" Paper presented at conference honoring Warren Bennis, Marine del Rey, May 6, 2000.

[6] Vrij, A. (2000) *Detecting Lies and Deceit: The Psychology of Lying and the Implications for Professional Practice* Chichester: John Wiley and Sons, page 217.

[7] Myths exist: there are those who still swear when someone does not look them fully in the eye, they are not telling the truth, but this is culturally and individually defined. One day, however, science may help much more than it currently does. Functional magnetic resonance imaging (FMRI) technologies, currently being developed, may one day get to the level where minds can be read.

[8] Flattery can be a feature of mendacious undermining, but an instinctive way to ensure survival and progress, as suggested by Richard Stengel. "Like all animals, chimps do whatever is best for their own genetic self-interest, and deception has proved to be an integral part of that self interest. A male chimp, after a clandestine sexual encounter with a female who is part of the alpha male's harem, will prostrate himself with extra fervour before the alpha male, who is unaware of what has taken place. Chimps seeking to topple the existing order will act deferential to the alpha male, while secretly forming alliances with other chimps. Male chimps vying for

group support in power struggles go out of their way to groom females and play with their infants – something they would not normally do..." p. 34 of *You're Too Kind* by Stengel, R. (2000) London: Pocket Books.

[9]   Berreby, D. (2005) *Us and Them: Understanding Your Tribal Mind* New York: Little, Brown page 16.

[10]   For a particularly insightful account of how bullying can be reduced at school, see Dweck, C (2006). *Mindset: The New Psychology of Success* New York Ballantine.

[11]   Tiedens, L. Z. (2001) "Anger and advancement versus sadness and subjugation: The effect of negative emotion expressions on social status conferral" *Journal of Personality and Social Psychology,* 80, 86-94.and Van Kleef, G.A. & Côté, S (2007). Expressing Anger in Conflict: When it Helps and When it Hurts *Journal of Applied Psychology,* 92: 1557-1569.

[12]   From Dunn, S. (*WebProNews*), June 10, 2002 *What's Going on With Mobbing, Bullying and Work Harassment* from BullyBusters.org:

[13]   Hornstein, H (1996) *Brutal Bosses and Their Prey* New York: Riverhead Books (G.P Putnam's Sons).

[14]   Conniff, Richard (2005) *The Ape in the Corner Office: Understanding the Workplace Beast in All of Us* New York: Crown Business pp. 77-78.

[15]   Forni, P.M., Buccino, D. L., Greene, R.E., Freedman, M.L., Stevens, D., Stack, T (2003) The Baltimore Incivility Study, retrieved from http://www.ubalt.edu/jfi/jfi/reports/civility.PDF

[16]   Forni, P.M., D.L. Buccino, R.E. Greene, N. M. Freedman, D. Stevens, T. Stack (2003) "The Baltimore Workplace Civility Study"

retrieved April 11, 2008 from http://www.ubalt.edu/jfi/jfi/reports/civility

[17] Field, T. (1996) *Bully Insight* retrieved from www.success unlimited.co.uk;www.bullyonline.org

[18] Carolan, L. (2004) *Costs Spiral as Stress Takes Toll in Workplace* The Birmingham Post (England), February 24.

[19] Andersson, L., & Pearson, C. (1999). "Tit for tat? The spiraling effect of incivility in the workplace." *Academy of Management Review*, 24: 452-471.

[20] I have often wondered at the propensity of certain activists to defend violence (often done by persons who hate) and give the perpetrators far more recognition than victims. For example, "A woman may respect, or even admire, a man who hates, but not a man who fears; a man seldom admires a woman who hates but he may respect a woman's fears." Lukacs, J (1997) *Fear and hatred*. American Scholar, 66 (3) p. 437. It is my own opinion that this feeling also leads to violence.

[21] A secondary victim in this context is an employee who has witnessed an act of violence rather than partaken in it. The act of witnessing may incur emotional and even physical problems.

[22] Centers for Disease Control and Prevention *Occupational Violence*, retrieved from http://www.cdc.gov/niosh/topics/violence/

[23] Kaufman, J. and Zigler, E. (1987) "Do abused children become abusive parents?" *American Journal of Orthopsychiatry*, 57: 186-192.

24 Teicher M H., Glod C. A., Surrey, J. & Swett C. (1993) Early childhood abuse and limbic system ratings in adult psychiatric outpatients. *Journal of Neuropsychiatry and Clinical Neurosciences* 5: 301-6.

25 Genetic Link to Violent Youth Behavior, *Science* 2 Aug. 2002. See also Salleh, A. for *Science Online* "Genes Linked to Violent Tendencies" Posted August 10, 2006.

26 Gilligan, J. (2001) *Preventing Violence* London: Thomas and Hudson p. 52-43.

27 There are 1.3 million incidents of work-related violence a year according to the British Crime survey. These incidents can result in physical injuries or anxiety and stress for the people affected. They also have serious consequences for their employers who have to deal with the resulting poor staff morale, high absenteeism, recruitment and staff turnover problems and poor business image http://findarticles.com/p/articles/mi_qa5428/is_/ai_n21322640

28 Adapted from St. Martin's University "Violence Policies", retrieved from http://www.stmartin.edu/Security/Policies/violence.html

CHAPTER 2

29 Lieberman, D. J. (2009) *Executive Power* New Jersey: John Wiley and Sons.

30 In most organizations, this virtually non-existent leadership leads to a delay in decision-making and an absence of feedback, leading to ambiguity concerning objectives, responsibilities, and

tasks. This style of leadership leads to role conflicts and interpersonal conflicts, often escalating the incidence of workplace bullying. Laissez faire leadership is usually accompanied by the condition of employees pretending to work, a skill that can be honed down to a fine art in companies where employees are openly or silently in conflict, or just don't care. Skogstad, A., Einarsen, S., Torsheim, T., Aasland, M.S. & Hetland, H. (2007) "The destructiveness of laissez-faire leadership behavior *Journal of Occupational Health Psychology*. 12 (1), 80-92.

31   Everyone can pretend to work...the French Book *Bonjour Paresse* by Corinne Maier, discusses the art of pretending to be working when you are not, in Rapaille, G.C. (2006) "Leveraging the psychology of the salesperson: A conversation with psychologist and anthropologist" *Harvard Business Review*: 84 (7/8), 42, 44-47, 186. There is also a Russian saying "they pretend to pay us, we pretend to work" which suggests at the very least that companies should look at how they are remunerating employees.

32   We do not necessarily embrace change because we are creatures of habit at the workplace. About 95% of behavior is habit-based, either unconsciously or consciously. (For more on this subject, See Schwartz, T. (2010) "The Way We're Working Isn't Working" New York: Simon and Schuster.

Depending on the situation, it might be useful for the CM to say that "let's go for a change that is worth the effort."

33   One of the problems with simplifying or "dumbing it down" as the popular term goes, is that many people have more respect for big words – in that case ask for permission to

speak very simply, and state that this is what you appreciate yourself.

34   A study of 1 million students conducted by the US College Board in the 70s, showed that 70% of students asked to rate themselves in comparison to their peers, said they were above-average in leadership ability. Regarding the ability to get along with others, 60% of the students rated themselves in the top decile, with 25% considering themselves in the top 1% - get real ref from Lovallo, D. & Kahneman, D. (2003) "Delusions of success: how optimism undermines executives' decisions" *Harvard Business Review*, 81, (7), 56-63.

35   Hammonds, K. H. (2002) "5 Habits of Highly Reliable Organizations" *Fast Company* 58 (3), 124-127.

36   "Organizations demand effective change leadership" *Blanchard Study Uncovers Organizational Challenges as Companies Prepare for More Turbulent Times Ahead* retrieved at http://www.kenblanchard.com/News_Events/Press_Releases/?id=1470

37   I'm unsure of the original author of SMARTER goals S = specific, M = measurable, A = achievable, R = realistic, T = time based, E = exiciting, R = resource based and recorded.

38   De Bono, E. (1999) *Six Thinking Hats* Boston: Little Brown and Company.

39   Root cause analysis takes place after an event has occurred, getting to its root causes rather than just the symptoms. The Balanced Scorecard is a performance measurement framework first developed by Robert Kaplan and David Norton.

They have written books and articles on the subject. TQM is a method which ensures that quality is a critical factor in every operation in the company. ISO produces international standards for public, private and civic organizations.

40 Pasmore, W (1994) *Creating Strategic Change: Designing the Flexible, High-Performing Organization* New York: John Wiley and Sons.

41 For an excellent book on this subject see Ichijo, K. and Nonaka, I. (2007) *Knowledge Creation and Management: New Challenges for Managers* New York: Oxford University Press.

42 A question like this may be asked to see if there has been an improvement over the years.

43 See, for example Livesley, W. J. (Ed.) (2001) Handbook of Personality Disorders: Theory, Research, and Treatment. New York: Guilford Press.

44 A particularly good article on WPV prevention is Centre for Disease Control: *Workplace Violence Prevention Strategies and Research Needs Report from the Conference - Partnering in Workplace Violence Prevention, translating research into practice* retrieved from http://www.cdc.gov/niosh/violcont.html

45 Many critical problems occur via this decision-route: change seemingly for its own sake has been done in organizations with ill effect. Others taking similar actions may say how many successes they have had with various decisions to engender positive organizational change. Few shout to the world their disappointments in life, unless it is in the context of making

our successes seem more impressive. Yet, despite the fact that we may know this intellectually, we may be so lured by what another company has done and want to follow it exactly. At the same time experience and a deep knowledge of one's own culture may allow a manager to make a decision very quickly: what worked for that organization *might* be able to work here with important modifications: but let me get more information first.

46 Durkheim, E. (1902-6) *Moral Education* The Free Press, 1961.

47 Greve, H. R. (2003) *Organizational Learning from Performance Feedback: A Behavioral Perspective on Innovation and Change* Cambridge University Press, 2003.

48 Hill, D. (2007) *Emotionomics: Winning Hearts and Minds* Edina, MN Adams Business and Professional page 10.

CHAPTER 3

49 See Tyler, T. R. "Procedural Strategies for Gaining Deference: Increasing Social Harmony or Creating False Consciousness?" in J. Darley, D. Messick, and T. Tyler (Eds.) Social influences on ethical behavior in organizations (pp.69-88). Mahwah, NJ: Erlbaum.

50 DeGeus, A. (1997) *The Living Company* Boston: Long View Publishing.

51 Standards of Conduct in the House of Lords (Chapter 4) retrieved from http://www.archive.official-documents.co.uk/document/cm49/4903/4903-04.htm

52 Bauer suggests that we cannot always successfully manage all

of our conflicts of interest: He states "The plain fact is that no human being can be trusted as much as under a conflict of interest as when there's no conflict. It isn't that people will always do the wrong thing; it isn't that we always put our private interests ahead of the public interest; it's just that if you have several, mutually conflicting wishes or interests, then you can't satisfy all of them...a television program ...a few years ago, showed many doctors, clinicians, researchers who thought it was quite all right to give speeches praising the value of a given drug even when the manufacturer of the drug was paying them to give the speech". Bauer H. H. (2001) *Ethics in Science* http://www.chem.vt.edu/ethics/habuer-intro.html

53   Emotional intelligence is further discussed in Chapter 7.

54   *Interests*-based is used as in a conflict of *interests*. Conflicts of interest are defined differently by different specialists – but in the workplace it is mostly about the distribution of various kinds of benefits and costs and divergent views with respect to appropriate trade-offs, from Noonan, J. (2004) "Need satisfaction and group conflict: beyond a rights-based approach *Social Theory and Practice*, 30 (2), 175-192.

55   Gleason, S. E. (1997) *Workplace Dispute Resolution: Directions for the 21st Century* Michigan State University Press, (page 85).

56   Note that this does not always indicate industrial action. Employees can disrupt an organization by various ways, including using all the various kinds of conflict described in Part 1.

57   Dorcey, A. H. J. (1986) *Bargaining in the Governance of Pacific*

Coastal Resources: Research and Reform Vancouver: Westwater Research Centre, University of British Columbia in Mitchell, B. (2004) (Ed.) *Resource and Environmental Management in Canada* Don Mills, Ontario: Oxford University Press.

58   Hawley, C. (2001) 100+ *Tactics for Office Politics* New York: Barrons p. 107.

59   Employees can boast after "winning" a case and this should be strongly discouraged, even as a way to protect the employee herself who may now be seen as too big for her boots.

60   U.S., Congress, House, Committee on Energy and Commerce, *Insider Trading: Hearings Before the Subcomm. on Telecommunications, Consumer Protection, and Finance*, 99th Cong., 2d sess., 1986, p. 76 (statement of Harvey L. Pitt). In Spencer, M. P. & Ronald R. Sims (1995) *Corporate Misconduct: The Legal, Societal, and Management Issues* Westport Connecticut: Quorum Books.

61   There are too many cases where employees falsely accuse other employees of sexually harassing them. I have also known of at least 20 cases where an employee makes a pass at someone who is not interested, and the rejected person's comment on the other's sexual preferences, which have a more serious impact on careers in some societies than others.

62   Byrne, J. A. (2003) "How to lead now: Getting Extraordinary Performance When You Can't Pay for It." *Fast Company*, 73, August, p. 62.

63   Government of British Columbia: The Future of Employee Learning: A Learning Strategy for the Public Service of British Columbia 2002 retrieved at page 5 http://www.bcpublic

service.ca/learning/pdf/Corporate%20Learning%20 Strategy.pdf

64   The reasons are "they don't know why they should do it, they don't know how to do it, they don't know what they're supposed to do, they think your way will not work, they think their way is better, they think something else is more important, there is no positive consequence to them for doing it, they think they are doing it, they are rewarded for not doing it, they are punished for doing what they're supposed to do, they anticipate a negative consequence for doing it, there is no negative consequence to them for poor performance, there are obstacles beyond their control, their personal limits prevent them from performing, personal problems, and no one could do it. Fournies, F. (2007) *Why Employees Don't Do What They are Supposed to Do* New Jersey McGraw Hill.

65   Hill, D. (2007) *Emotionomics* Edina, MN: Adams Business and Professional p. 269.

66   Henschel, P. (2001) "Understanding and winning the never-ending Search for talent" Retrieved from http://www.linezine. com/6.2/articles/phuwnes.htm

67   When employees are relaxed (such as a staff party or eating at the canteen) managers often engage in important non-focused conversations with them. The manager hears employees' views on a number of non-work and work related issues which also guide the leader as to their views towards how they learn about challenging interpersonal relationships. I have heard of one CEO who sometimes played dominoes with his staff: interestingly that organization was very profitable.

That bonding might have contributed to the organization's financial health.

[68] Yuncai Chen, Y., Dubé, C. M. Rice, C. J. Baram. T. Z. (2008) Rapid loss of dendritic spines after stress involves derangement of spine dynamics by corticotropin-releasing hormone *The Journal of Neuroscience* 28 (11), 2903-2911.

[69] There are normally four levels of evaluation (1) Reaction – the learner's opinion on the training (2) Learning – what knowledge, skills and attitudes did the learner gain (3) Behaviors: what new skills and knowledge is the learner applying to the job (4) Results: did the learner transfer the necessary knowledge and skills to the workplace, and if so, what results were achieved that are aligned with the organization's goals.

[70] Market share is an important determinant in profitability, return on assets is an accounting measure of an organization's profitability and stock return is appreciation of equity value.

[71] The HSE document on Violence at Work: A Guide for Employers is a useful guide for any learning program and can be at http://www.hse.gov.uk/pubns/indg69.pdf Also go to http://www.countrydoctor.co.uk/education/education %20-%20HSE,%20violence%20at%20work.htm for information on copies on the national work standards for managing work-related violence.

[72] Conniff, R. (2005) *The Ape in the Corner Office: Understanding the Workplace Beast in All of Us* New York: Crown Business p. 114-115 and 146-147.

73   Carlson, R. (1998) *Don't Sweat the Small Stuff at Work* New York: Hyperion p.93.

74   It is best to say little about one's colleagues that is not work related in any environment much less in a dysfunctional environment that is an equal-opportunity environment for truth, half truths and untruths. A relative of mine got to a high position in his profession by just listening to the negative things that others had to say. He never added an opinion, and whether he liked the person or not, he said nothing.

75   I think that this is a word everyone should know. It means pleasure at the downfall of another human being. Portman (2000: 198) states "The moral problem of Schadenfreude is threefold. First, there is widespread confusion about the normative moral acceptability of taking pleasure in the suffering of a person whose *contretemps* is either trivial or a result of having trespassed justice. Second, this confusion over the normative status of Schadenfreude may give rise to self-deceitful attempts to persuade ourselves that we take pleasure in the knowledge that another suffers, as opposed to taking pleasure in the actual suffering itself. Third, this same confusion no doubt invites mental efforts to rationalize as justified the suffering we fear or otherwise cannot under-stand. Portmann, J. (2000) *When Bad Things Happen to Other People* New York: Routledge p. 198.

76   Ronson, J. (2011) *The Psychopath Test: A Journey Through the Madness Industry* New York: Riverhead Books p. 113.

77   Stout, M. (2005) *The Sociopath Next Door* New York: Broad-way Books Page 87.

[78] Epstein; J. (2003) *Envy* New York: Oxford University Press. The quote is on page 92.

[79] Moran, S. & Scgweutzerm M. E. (2000). "When better is worse: envy and the use of deception" *Negotiation and Conflict Management Research* 1 (1), 3-30.

[80] Duran, P. L. & Nasci, D (2000) *Tactical attitude: learn from powerful real-life experience* New York: Looseleaf Law Publications. This quote is on page 33.

[81] Grossman, D with Christensen, L. W. (2007) *On Combat: The Psychology and Physiology of Deadly Conflict in War and in Peace* p. 183 Warrior Science Publications.

CHAPTER 5

[82] A study looked at the positive effects of a "depression coach" on elderly people with depression. The death rate fell by an average of 45 per cent among those who had someone to talk to (the coach gave them a reason to live), and the rate of deaths fell from 89 per 1000 person years to 20.6 deaths Gallo, J. J. , Bogner, H.R.,Morales, K. H., Post, E.P., Lin, J. Y. & Bruce, M. L. (2007) "The Effect of a Primary Care Practice-Based Depression Intervention in Older Adults: A Randomized Trial" *Annals of Internal Medicine*, 146, 689-98.

[83] Niederhoffer, K. G. & Pennebaker, J. W. "Sharing one's story: on the benefits of talking about emotional experience" Chapter 41 in Snyder, C. R. & Lopez, S. J. (2005) *Handbook of Positive Psychology* New York: Oxford University Press pp. 573-583.

84 Of note, the indication is that aggression control therapy is quite interesting to assist violent patients to reduce their high levels of anger. See Hornsveld, R. H., Nijman, H.L., Hollin, C. R., & Kraaimaat, F. W (2008). "Aggression Control Therapy for violent forensic psychiatric patients: method and clinical practice. *International Journal of Offender Therapy and Comparative Criminology,* 52, pp. 222-233. Note that this therapy was provided for patients for personality disorders.

85 Niederhoffer, K. G. & Pennebaker, J. W. "Sharing one's story: on the benefits of talking about emotional experience." Chapter 41 in Snyder, C. R. & Lopez, S. J. (2005) *Handbook of Positive Psychology* New York: Oxford University Press pp. 573-583 Quotation pp. 582.

86 EMDR is one of these fascinating methods, which has received a lot of attention. Developed by Francine Shapiro, it requires an extensive protocol. In some of the phases of the treatment, movement of the finger and other techniques is used while the client focuses on an image or a thought: then the client is asked to describe what has happened. Shapiro states: "The client learns what is useful about the past experience, and the event is restored in memory in an adaptive, healthy, non-distressing form" (p.2). The client learns that she is not a slave to these emotions, and a more hopeful future becomes attainable. Shapiro, F. (2001) *Eye Movement Desensitization and Reprocessing: Basic Principles, Protocols, and Procedures* New York: The Guilford Press.

87 Swanson, J., Holzer, C., Ganju, V., Jono, R. (1990). Violence and psychiatric disorder in the community: Evidence from the

epidemiologic catchment area surveys. *Hospital and Community Psychiatry* 41 (7), 761-770.

[88] Perspectives: Managing Coaching for Results and ROI retrieved from http://www.kenblanchard.com/Business_ Leadership/Effective_Leadership_White_Papers/Managing_ Coaching_Results_ROI/

[89] Tennen, H., & Affleck, G. "Benefit finding and benefit-reminding" Chapter 42 in *Handbook of Positive Psychology* Snyder, C.R. & Lopez, Shane, J (2005) New York: Oxford University Press p. 584-597.

[90] Norem, J. K. (2001) *The Positive Power of Negative Thinking* Cambridge, Massachusetts, Basic Books.

[91] See Holland, J. & Lewis, S. (Eds.) (2000) *The Human Side of Cancer, Living with Hope, Coping with Uncertainty*, New York: Harper Collins and Coyne JC Stefanek M Steven Palmer C, Psychotherapy and Survival in Cancer: The Conflict Between Hope and Evidence, Psychological Bulletin 2007, 133, (3), 367–394.

[92] Stockdale, J. (1995) *Thoughts of a Philosophical Fighter Pilot* Sanford: Hoover Institution and Stockdale, J. (1984) *A Vietnam Experience: Ten Years of Reflection*, Sanford: Hoover Institution, Stanford.

[93] Optimism is a precursor to good results, but it can be over-done. Barbara Ehrenreich states that a study coauthored by Martin Seligman showed that pessimists were less likely to fall into depression following a negative life event such as the

death of a family member. In Ehrenreich, B. (2009) *Bright-Sided: How the Relentless Promotion of Positive Thinking has Undermined America* New York: Metropolitan Books. My experience indicates that this may also be true of great managers – they may articulate optimism but secretly are realists – seeing both the good and bad aspects of a decision or action.

[94] Simon, Robert I. (1996) Bad Men Do What Good Men Dream: A Forensic Psychiatrist Illuminates the Darker Side of Human Behavior American Psychiatric Press page 3. He also states: "What about the good people among us? Most humans go about the daily business of life without robbing, raping, or committing murder. Yet after 32 years of work as a treating and as a forensic psychiatrist, I am absolutely convinced that there is no great gulf between the mental life of the common criminal and that of the everyday, upright citizen. The dark side exists in all of us. There is no "we-they" dichotomy between the good citizens, the "we", and the criminals, the "they". Who among us has not had the wish or felt the urge to do something illicit? If we could press a button and eliminate our rivals or enemies with impunity, how many of us would resist? In fact, probably very few people would be left standing if this were possible."

[95] Someone who wanted society's approval also stated that society's views was nothing in comparison with God's views, found a way to rationalize his hard hitting stance at the workplace. He also stated that he had never forgotten a minister saying to him when he was young that God might reward "bad" people here on earth so that He would not afterwards:

"It's not that you hate anybody but you just have to step on people to get ahead. You can always make up for it later by praying to God for forgiveness." I told him I appreciated his honesty, but asked him gently if he did not think that God knew of his plan.

96 Tavris, C. & Aronson, E. (2007) *Mistakes were made: but not by me* Orlando: Harcourt p. 2.

97 Selgiman, M. (2011) *Flourish: A Visionary New Understanding of Happiness and Well-being* New York: Simon and Schuster page 2.

98 As Cialdini discussed so well, the reciprocity rule suggests that we comply with each other's requests.

99 Darley, J.M. & Latané, B. (1968) Bystander intervention in emergencies: diffusion of responsibility *Journal of Personality and Social Psychology*, 8, 377-383.

100 By Michael Kinsman, Copley News Service From California Job Journal: retrieved from http://www.jobjournal.com/article_full_text.asp?artid=1953

CHAPTER 6
101 World Health Organization retrieved from http://www.who.int/suggestions/faq/en/

102 Wellness is virtually interchangeable for health when used in organizations or schools.

103 For Omega 3 studies and other ways to reduce hypertension, a valuable book filled with citations of research studies is Whelton, P.K., He, J., Louis, G.T., (Eds.) (2003) *Lifestyle*

Modification for the Prevention and Treatment of Hypertension New York: Marcel Dekker.

[104] Zellner D. A., Loaiza S., Gonzalez Z., Pita J, Morales J., Pecora, D., Wolf, A. (2006) "Food selection changes under stress" *Physiology and Behavior* 87: 789–793.

[105] See Richardson, A. J. (2002) "The potential role of fatty acids in developmental dyspraxia." *The Dyspraxia Foundation Professional Journal* No. 1 Oxford University scientists found a link between children eating diets high in processed foods (i.e. junk foods) and underachievement. Junk foods are deficient in vitamins, minerals and essential fatty acids that boost brain power. Children with concentration and behavioral problems who were given omega 3 essential fats made significant improvements in reading, spelling, and concentration.

[106] ***Gesch, C. B., Hammond, S. M., Hampson, S. E., Eves, A., & Crowder, M. J.*** *(2002) "Influence of supplementary vitamins, minerals and essential fatty acids on the antisocial behavior of young adult prisoners"* **The British Journal of Psychiatry** *181: 22-28.*

[107] Kamp Jurriaan, O. "Can diet help stop depression and violence?" Posted August 28, 2007. *Corporate Performance* www.corporatepa.com

[108] Taking too many multivitamins may be increase the risk for prostate cancers. See "Heavy Multivitamin Use May Be Linked to Advanced Prostate Cancer" *Journal of the National Cancer Institute,* May 16, 2007 retrieved from http://www.natap .org/2007/HIV/052207_09.htm

109 Pema, R. & Monto, K. "Neurophysiology: basis for the benefits of exercise on physical and mental health", 51 (34) Source: PsycCRITIQUES.

110 See for example Ray, U. S., Mukhopadhyaya, S., Purkayastha, S. S., Asnani, V., Tomer, O. S., Prashad, R. et al. (2001). "Effects of yogic exercises on physical and mental health of young fellowship course trainees" *Indian Journal of Physiological Pharmocology,* 45(1), 37-53, and Annesi J.J. Changes in Depressed Mood Associated with 10 Weeks of Moderate Cardiovascular Exercise in Formerly Sedentary Adults. Psychological Reports (June 2005): 96, (3): 855-62.

111 Callaghan, P. (2004) "Exercise: a neglected intervention in mental health care?" *Journal of Psychiatric and Mental Health Nursing* 11 (4), 476-483.

112 Johnson, A., O'Brien, J., Dahlke. L (2006) "The effect of an acute exercise bout on academic performance of kinesiology undergraduate students" *Journal of Undergraduate Kinesiology Research.* 1 (2), 23-30.

113 See Okonski, V. O. (2003) "Exercise as a counseling intervention" *Journal of Mental Health Counseling,* 25 (1).

114 **Cahn**, B. R. & Polich, J. (2006) "Meditation states and traits: EEG, ERP, and neuroimaging studies." *Psychological Bulletin* 132, (2), 180-211.

115 Schneider, R., Nidich, S., Kotchen, J. M., Kotchen, T., Grim, C., Rainforth, M., King, C. G., Salerno, J. (2009) "Effects of stress reduction on clinical events in African Americans with coronary

heart disease: A randomized controlled trial." *Circulation* 120: S461.

[116] Dillbeck M., C. Banus, C. Polanzi and G. Landrith. 1988. "Test of a field model of consciousness and social change." *Journal of Mind and Behavior,* 9 (4), 457-486.

[117] Adapted from IBID.

[118] Shapiro, S.L., G.E.R. Schwartz & C. Santerre (2005) "Meditation and positive psychology" In Snyder, C. R. & Lopez, S.J. (Eds) *Handbook of Positive Psychology* Oxford University Press.

[119] Hall, P.D. (1999) The effect of meditation on the academic performance of African American college students *Journal of Black Studies,* 29 (3), 251-265.

[120] Smith, C. S. & Sulsky, L. (1995). "An investigation of job-related coping strategies across multiple stressors and samples." in Murphy, L. R., Hurell Jr., J. J., Sauter, S. L. Keita, G. P. (Eds.), *Job Stress Intervention* (pp. 109-123). Washington, D.C: American Psychological Association.

[121] Kraft, U. (2006) "Burned out" *Scientific American Mind* 17 (3): 29-33 p. 31.

[122] For example Wertz, A.T.., Ronda, J.M.., Czeisler, C. A., Wright, K.P. (2006) "Effects of sleep inertia on cognition" *Journal of the American Medical Association* Vol. 295 (2) pp. 163-164 and Dawson, D, Reid, K. (1997) "Fatigue, alcohol and performance impairment" *Nature;* 388: 235.

[123] Grossman, D. (2007) *On Combat: The Psychology and Physiology of Deadly Conflict in War and Peace* Millstadt, IL Warrior Science Publications.

124   Hamilton, N. A., Gallagher, M. W., Preacher, K. J., Stevens, N., Nelson, C. A., Karlson, C., & McCurdy, D. (2007) "Insomnia and well-being" *Journal of Consulting and Clinical Psychology* 75 (6), 939-946.

125   Baranski, J. V. (2007) "Fatigue, sleep loss, and confidence in judgment" *Journal of Experimental Psychology*: 13 (4): 182-196.

126   Goleman, D. (1998) *Working with Emotional Intelligence* New York: Bantam p. 317.

127   Goleman, D. (1995). *Emotional Intelligence.* New York: Bantam Books.

128   Also see Cherniss, C. & Goleman, D. (Eds) *The Emotionally Intelligent Workplace: How to Select for, Measure and Improve Emotional Intelligence in Individuals, Groups and Organizations* San Fransisco: Jossey-Bass/Wiley.

129   **Ilangovan, A.**, **Scroggins, W. A.**, & **Rozell, E. J**. (2007) Managerial Perspectives on Emotional Intelligence Differences Between India and the United States: The Development of Research Propositions **International Journal of Management** 24 (3), 541-548.

130   EQ means Emotional quotient.

131   Potsky, M. (2006) *Talent Smart: The Business Case for Emotional Intelligence,* retrieved from *www.talentsmart.com*

132   Tavuchis, N. (1991) *Mea Culpa: A Sociology of Apology and Reconciliation* Stanford University Press.

133   The Bible has varying views on forgiveness - a minister reminded me the other day of Romans 12:18, "If it is possible, as far as

it depends on you, live at peace with everyone." Not being at peace with everyone of course suggests that the person is not able to forgive.

134 A number of interesting studies testifying to this fact are found in Richman, J. M. and Franser, M. W (Eds.) (2001) *The Context of Youth Violence: Resilience, Risk, and Protection*. Westport, CT: Praeger.

135 Baier, C. J., & Wright, B. R. E. (2001). "If you love me, keep my commandments: A meta-analysis of the effect of religion on crime." *Journal of Research in Crime and Delinquency*, 38: 3-21.

136 I have avoided using the word religion, though spirituality is often associated with religion. Religious practice can have enormous benefits such as feeling unity with the creator and love, but the studies here are also interesting. For example, several studies indicate that religiousness is more strongly related to sexual restraint among females than among males: economic crimes may be an exception to this rule, especially among executives who abuse their authority. See Paloutzian, R.F. & Park, C.L. (Eds.) *Handbook of the Psychology of Religion and Spirituality*. New York: Guilford Press.

137 See for example, Bennett, M.P. & Lengacher, C. (2008) "Humor and laughter may influence health" *Evidence-based Complementary and Alternative Medicine*, 5 (1), 17:37-40 Oxford University Press.

138 See Gladwell, M. (2008) *Outliers: The Story of Success* New York: Little, Brown and Company. The quote is on page 7.

139 Employees should be active within reason, depending on their stress and work schedules. Of note, according to the Canadian Mental Health Association, 58% of Canadians feel overloaded by their multiple roles such as work, home and family, friends, volunteer and community service Canadian Mental Health Association retrieved at http://www.cmha.ca/bins/print_page.asp?cid=284-294-295-313&lang=1

140 Csikszentmihalyi, M., & Csikszentmihalyi, I. S. (2006) *A Life Worth Living* New York: Oxford University Press.

141 Google from all accounts seem to be a fascinating place to work, a place in which innovators can feel comfortable. "Sameness" does not appear to be a value. I suspect that tolerance of others is a great value of that company.

142 "What's more," says Csikszentmihalyi, "the openness and sensitivity of creative people can expose them to suffering and pain." As electrical engineer Jacob Rabinow told Csikszentmihalyi (author of the groundbreaking book Flow), "Inventors have a low threshold of pain. Things bother them. And yet, few things in life bring more satisfaction and fulfillment than the process of creation." From Hara Estroff Marano (2007) "The myth that madness heightens creative genius." *Psychology Today*, retrieved from http://www.webmd.com/bipolar-disorder/features/genius-and-madness. Also see "Scientists have wondered for a long time why madness and creativity seem linked, particularly in artists, musicians, and writers," notes Shelley Carson, a Harvard psychologist. "Our research results indicate that low levels of latent inhibition and exceptional

flexibility in thought predispose people to mental illness under some conditions and to creative accomplishments under others."

Cromie, W. J. (2003) "Creativity tied to mental illness" Harvard Gazette: October.

[143] Inspirers may become discouraged when others are not easily inspired. Inspirers would be like salesmen, and would be taught to have resilience and to be positive in the face of negativity.

CHAPTER 7

[144] Tichy, Noel M. and Bennis, W. G. (2007) "Making judgment calls, the ultimate act of leadership" *Harvard Business Review*, 85 (10), 94-107. This quote is on p. 94.

[145] This was the Values in Action Character Strengths survey. Up to the time of this writing, the survey is free of cost. Go to http://www.viastrengths.org/

[146] See the article by Wrzesniewski, A & Hutton, J. E. (2001) "Crafting a job: revisioning employees as active crafters of their work." *Academy of Management Review* 26 (2), 179-201.

[147] An excellent book on this subject is by Walton, D (2008) *Informal Logic: A Pragmatic Approach* New York: Cambridge University Press. This book discusses issues such as relevance, appeals to emotion, personal attacks, straw man arguments, jumping to conclusions and uses and abuses of expert opinion.

[148] Wegner, D. M. (1997) "When the antidote is the poison: ironic mental control process" *Psychological Science* 8 (3), 148-150.

149   Goleman, D. (2003) *Destructive Emotions: A Scientific Dialogue with the Dalai Lama* Bantam Books.

150   Cloke, K. & Goldsmith, J. (2005) *Resolving Conflicts at Work* San Francisco: Jossey-Bass.

151   Ben-Shahar, T. (2007) *Happier: Learn the Secrets to Learn the Secrets to Daily Joy and Lasting Fulfillment* New York:: McGraw Hill p. 163.

152   Fisher, R. & Shapiro, D. (2005) *Beyond Reason: Using Emotions as You Negotiate* New York: Viking p. 13.

153   Goleman, D. & Boyatzis, R. (2008) "Social intelligence and the biology of leadership", *Harvard Business Review*, Vol. 86 (9) pp. 74, 76-81. The quote is on p. 76.

154   I first used the technique when I roomed with a complete stranger when we were abroad for a 6-week course. All of us of course wanted our own rooms, but we found ourselves in a situation where we had to share a small room. I said to the other lady "we don't know each other, but I really want to know what annoys you and what doesn't and I will tell you mine." She was too polite at first to share her "don'ts" but when I told her I don't like loud music, and if you need to play it, give me warning, she readily gave me her list of annoyances as well. We were the only two of eighteen roommates who did not have some form of fuss or argument during our stay.

About the Author

D r. Angela Ramsay is a Commonwealth Scholar who is a consultant in the following areas: instructional design, organization development, and environmental health and safety. She is a certified professional mediator and also a certified 6 Sigma Black Belt in quality management. She has worked as a consultant with UNESCO and UNICEF, The International Council of Adult Education, Ministry of Education/The Inter-American Development Bank, The International Labour Organization, and The Commonwealth Secretariat in London. Among her assignments during the past four years is her completion of the first draft of the International Labour Organization's HIV/AIDS policy for Educational Institutions in the Caribbean. She is also one of the architects of the Protocol for the Recruitment of British Commonwealth teachers, and developed a guide for the Professional Development of Commonwealth teachers in 54 countries. Dr. Ramsay has also worked for a number of private organizations.

www.ingramcontent.com/pod-product-compliance
Lightning Source LLC
Chambersburg PA
CBHW031201270326
41931CB00006B/355